Praise for Ove

From one overwhelmed mom to (probably) another, go buy five copies of this book ASAP. Read one, keep a backup, and give three to friends who will probably cry tears of gratitude. It's *that* good. Funny, poignant, godly, helpful—Jamie has knocked it out of the park again with this gem!
JESSICA SMARTT
Author of *Come On Home* and *Memory-Making Mom*

Overwhelmed Mom is the insightful companion every weary mother needs. With warmth, wisdom, and hard-won experience, Jamie Erickson offers not just advice but real-life encouragement for women in the thick of motherhood. Each chapter feels like a conversation with a trusted friend who truly understands the weight you carry and wants to help you lighten the load. Jamie's honest reflections and actionable tips will help you reclaim your time, talents, and peace. If you're ready to trade striving for consistency and peace, this book will lead the way.
JENNIFER PEPITO
Author of *Habits for a Sacred Home*

Overwhelmed Mom is a lifeline for the weary woman who feels like she's drowning in the demands of motherhood. Jamie Erickson beautifully combines practical wisdom with deep biblical encouragement, reminding readers that peace is possible—even in the middle of chaos. Her words are honest, relatable, and full of grace. I found myself nodding along, feeling both seen and gently challenged to refocus on what truly matters.
CRYSTAL PAINE
Mom of six, *New York Times* bestselling author, and founder of MoneySavingMom.com

If you have felt the weight of motherhood pushing you to your limits, *Overwhelmed Mom* by Jamie Erickson is a gift. Jamie faithfully reminds moms that we are not victims of motherhood; rather, we are empowered and equipped by God to raise our children for His glory. This book is steeped in biblical truth and refreshingly practical, offering real-life wisdom for moms when we need it most. I can't wait to share it with my friends!

WHITNEY NEWBY

Mother of four and author of *Lift Your Eyes*

Quiet the Chaos, Mind What Matters,
and Enjoy Your Life Again

JAMIE ERICKSON

MOODY PUBLISHERS

CHICAGO

© 2025 by
Jamie Erickson

All rights reserved. No part of this book may be reproduced in any form without permission in writing from the publisher, except in the case of brief quotations embodied in critical articles or reviews.

Scripture quotations, unless otherwise marked, are from the ESV® Bible (The Holy Bible, English Standard Version®), © 2001 by Crossway, a publishing ministry of Good News Publishers. Used by permission. All rights reserved. The ESV text may not be quoted in any publication made available to the public by a Creative Commons license. The ESV may not be translated in whole or in part into any other language.

Scripture quotations marked (NIV) are taken from the Holy Bible, New International Version®, NIV®. Copyright © 1973, 1978, 1984, 2011 by Biblica, Inc.™ Used by permission of Zondervan. All rights reserved worldwide. www.zondervan.com The "NIV" and "New International Version" are trademarks registered in the United States Patent and Trademark Office by Biblica, Inc.™

Scripture quotations marked (NKJV) are taken from the New King James Version®. Copyright © 1982 by Thomas Nelson. Used by permission. All rights reserved.

Names and details of some stories have been changed to protect the privacy of individuals.

Edited by Annette LaPlaca
Interior design: Puckett Smartt
Cover design: Kaylee Lockenour Dunn
Author photo: Dain Erickson

Library of Congress Cataloging-in-Publication Data
Names: Erickson, Jamie (Homeschool teacher) author
Title: Overwhelmed mom : calm the chaos, mind what matters, and enjoy your life again / Jamie Erickson.
Description: Chicago : Moody Publishers, [2025] | Includes bibliographical references. | Summary: "Overwhelmed Mom shows us how to push back against the weariness epidemic that plagues so many women. Through biblical principles and flexible solutions, Jamie helps us learn to make adjustments to our homes, schedules, and attitudes so that we may experience freedom and enjoy the gift of motherhood"-- Provided by publisher.
Identifiers: LCCN 2025012113 (print) | LCCN 2025012114 (ebook) | ISBN 9780802427984 paperback | ISBN 9780802476289 ebook
Subjects: LCSH: Motherhood--Religious aspects--Christianity | Well-being--Religious aspects--Christianity
Classification: LCC BV4529.18 .E753 2025 (print) | LCC BV4529.18 (ebook) | DDC 248.8/431--dc23/eng/20250516
LC record available at https://lccn.loc.gov/2025012113
LC ebook record available at https://lccn.loc.gov/2025012114

Originally delivered by fleets of horse-drawn wagons, the affordable paperbacks from D. L. Moody's publishing house resourced the church and served everyday people. Now, after more than 125 years of publishing and ministry, Moody Publishers' mission remains the same— even if our delivery systems have changed a bit. For more information on other books (and resources) created from a biblical perspective, go to www.moodypublishers.com or write to:

Moody Publishers
820 N. LaSalle Boulevard
Chicago, IL 60610

1 3 5 7 9 10 8 6 4 2

Printed in the United States of America

To Mama,
You may not remember, but I'll never forget

Contents

Chapter 1: Mind Your Business   9
Chapter 2: Narrate a Good Story   21
    The Motherload: Prayer Life   36
Chapter 3: Edit with Intention   41
    The Motherload: Decluttering   59
Chapter 4: Live in Your Season   63
    The Motherload: Shopping & Errands   75
Chapter 5: Choose Your Hard   79
    The Motherload: Menu Planning   97
Chapter 6: Just Start   103
    The Motherload: Cooking & Food Management   116
Chapter 7: Move the Needle   121
    The Motherload: Cleaning & Organizing   143
Chapter 8: Gather the Right People   147
    The Motherload: Holidays & Special Occasions   162
Chapter 9: Let Them Go to Let Them Grow   167
    The Motherload: Miscellaneous Management   187
Chapter 10: Loosen Your Grip   189
    Acknowledgments   197
    Notes   199

1

Mind Your Business

Chaos shouldn't be the norm, and while we can't always change the source of the chaos, we must tend to what we can change.
LYSA TERKEURST

"When will this year end?" I said as I stared at my phone, tears running in rivers down my cheeks. It was five-ish on some random Tuesday night. Instead of chopping tomatoes for the taco dinner I was supposed to be dishing up to my family momentarily, I was sending a video message of despair to three of my closest friends. The previous Friday evening, a deer had made a rather untimely leap onto the highway right in front of my husband's oncoming vehicle. The gently used car we had purchased just two months before was totaled. Unfortunately, so was the deer.

To make matters worse, three days after the carnage, our insurance company informed us of a small loophole in our policy that rendered our losses even greater. We would not be completely reimbursed for the car but would instead have to take a $5,000 loss. Did I mention that this was not just our primary car but our only car?

I reminded my friends that the accident was the latest in a series of disasters that seemed to define 2022 for us. "Let's rewind the tape for a second, shall we?" I said, discouragement and overwhelm lacing through every word. I began to inventory my year to them in a way that amplified the tragedies and completely dismissed the triumphs.

Due to a contract expiration at the end of the previous fiscal period, my self-employed husband lost one of his biggest clients, sending our finances into a tailspin for nearly six months. My mother's dementia diagnosis advanced rapidly, and she no longer recognized my voice right away when I called to check on her. Her physical and emotional care was taking its toll on all four of her daughters, including me. In August, one of my older sisters, who had been like a second mother to me for most of my life, lost her seven-year battle with breast cancer. Overcome with grief, I made my way across the country to deliver the eulogy at her funeral. Only a month later, I launched my second book out into the world. In the midst of parties, radio interviews, and social media appearances, I should have felt elated. Instead, I felt numb. I was in crisis fatigue, burdened by the cumulative effects of chronic stress.

"And the hits keep coming. Now we are car-less. Second verse, same as the first," I muttered under my breath, quietly waving the white flag of surrender as I hit "send" on my message. It was only October, but I was more than ready to pull the plug on the entire year.

I wish I could say that 2022 was an isolated season of bedlam. It wasn't. My adult life has been fraught with pressures of all kinds. There was the year when a dangerous cocktail of immaturity and inexperience led to a kitchen fire in my newlywed apartment, forcing my husband and me into a renovation project we were not financially prepared to tackle. Then, there was the year my dad had five strokes. A heart attack capped off that tumultuous spell and eventually took his life. A handful of years later, when we had four kids, all under five, our hot water heater decided to boycott. Until we could afford to repair it, we spent over a month boiling bucket after bucket of water like we were playing a real-life game of Oregon Trail. And who could forget the year our recently remodeled basement flooded just two days before we were to host out-of-state relatives for an entire week? Perhaps the most difficult of all was the year our daughter had a heart attack and was airlifted to a pediatric ICU several hours away. Hospital stints, long-distance trips to cardiac specialists, and an eventual surgery left us all feeling emotionally and physically fragile.

Couple all of these acute seasons of mayhem with the brain-breaking business of everyday living—the laundry piles, the dentist appointments, the meal prep, the errands, the bills, the work meetings, the sports team fundraisers, the field trips, the volunteer committees, the random spam calls from Indonesia regarding the extended warranty to a vehicle I didn't actually own—and I had the makings of a life that, at times, looked like one giant game of whack-a-mole.

The year 2022 seemed different, though. It came with wave after wave of disaster, all threatening to pull me under. I spent most of that year just dog-paddling, trying not to drown in the deep end.

Buried by Busy

Even as I stood sweat-panicking in my kitchen that fateful evening, rehearsing the year's events out loud in front of the screen while pressing my palms into my eyes to stop the torrent of tears, I knew I wasn't the only one who felt frayed by the past twelve months. The three women on the other side of that group message had stood on the knife's edge of disaster also. They, too, had clambered up a few jagged ridges, barefoot with no rope. Not even counting the reverberating effects of a pandemic, their days had been riddled with struggles of all kinds.

What's more, I had tangible proof that white-knuckle moments went far beyond the four of us. Overwhelming days are universal.

Sitting at the bottom of my dresser drawer, tucked safely under a pile of well-worn T-shirts, was a stack of 3x5 cards—each a simple declaration of distress. I had collected them from women across the country who had attended a Q&A session at a family conference where I had been invited to speak. Each mom in attendance was given a blank index card and was asked to write down her burning questions about marriage, motherhood, faith, friendship, or any other piece of a woman's world that came to mind. Several of the cards were randomly selected and read aloud by a moderator. The three panelists, myself included, were expected to provide unrehearsed answers to the waiting crowd.

Every question said the same thing: **Help! I'm overwhelmed—overworked and understaffed.**

Dozens and dozens of questions came pouring in.

"Some days, it gets to be too much—the endless cooking, laundry piles, constant questions, and bickering. What do you do when you're buried by *busy*, and you're tempted to jump in your car and drive far, far away from it all?"

"Most days, I am so emotionally and mentally spent by the time my husband gets home from work. How can I ensure that I have enough 'me' left for him while also not feeling like a crazy lady?"

"How do you steer home, school, and work without sinking all three ships at the same time?"

"I'm only one person. How can I meet everyone's needs when I'm so outnumbered? What about my needs?"

Every question was worded differently from all the others, but without fail, they all said the same thing: *Help! I'm overwhelmed—overworked and understaffed.*

Perhaps you can relate. Maybe as you're reading this, you are making a mental inventory of the questions you'd love to submit anonymously to a panel of peers someday. Possibly you, too, are wondering why life didn't come with a warning label. *Caution: flash flood zone, enter at your own risk.* I understand, friend. If an organization were dedicated to threading difficult needles, my name would be on the letterhead. So would yours. So would the names of all the women who attended the conference session. Because you see, *struggle* is synonymous with *humanity*. We can't outrun crisis. It is one of the continuous ripples of the fall.

Jesus put it this way in John 16:33: "I have told you these things, so that in me you may have peace. In this world you will have trouble. But take heart! I have overcome the world" (NIV). If we were looking for advance notice about the turbulent days ahead, we'd have to admit that Christ couldn't have made His warning clearer. It's splashed across the pages of Scripture in bright red letters.

> **Struggle is synonymous with humanity.**

The Path to Peace

But while *struggle* is unavoidable, feelings of overwhelm don't have to define our days. Peace is possible, even when it feels like the sky is falling. Admittedly, that message can be a hard pill to swallow, especially when the sin scars of this world seem to riddle our lives with so much difficulty.

As I stood at the counter shoving fistfuls of lettuce and cheese into waiting taco shells that night in 2022, the very idea of claiming calm amid all my chaos made me flinch. *When will Your overcoming start in my life, Lord?* I silently prayed. *When will I experience Your promised peace?* It felt like His words were aimed at everyone but me.

A few days later, while I was cocooned in a blanket on my favorite comfy chair, with my Bible in hand, my eyes fell on some verses that began to soften the brittle edges of my heart. The Lord, in His kindness, drew me to 1 Thessalonians 4:11–12—verses that I had read numerous times before, but that took on a new, vibrant glow in those dark days.

In what is believed to be his very first letter to the newly formed church, exhorting the believers of Thessalonica (a northern city in ancient Greece) to brotherly love, the apostle Paul wrote, "Make it your ambition to lead a quiet life: You should mind your own business and work with your hands, just as we told you, so that your daily life may win the respect of outsiders and so that you will not be dependent on anybody" (NIV). The "quiet life" mentioned here is *hēsychazō* in Greek and is exclusively used in reference to keeping one's peace in the midst of difficult circumstances and embracing the restorative rest of the Sabbath.[1]

Peace and rest—if that duo is not the very opposite of overwhelm, I'm not sure what is.

Tucked safely in the middle of this lengthy letter to the church, Paul gave the two-fold prescription for living the quiet life: mind your own business, and work with your hands.

You see, it had been brought to Paul's attention that some Christ followers were abandoning their daily responsibilities and surviving on the charity of fellow believers. They were meddling in the affairs of others and sitting idle. To some extent, their lack of peace and rest was self-inflicted.

While our contemporary minds can read *mind your own business* in harsh tones, with a degree of snark included, Paul's admonition to "mind your own business" was meant to ensure that church members could continue to love each other generously, as they were known to do. They were to give and receive communal aid to one another whenever appropriate but were encouraged not to stir up trouble or take advantage of others. Moreover, in a culture that viewed manual labor as menial, the simple directive to "work with your hands" declared to their Greco-Roman neighbors that labor, when done sincerely, was honorable. Their Christian commitment to walk uprightly created curiosity in the surrounding community and compelled unbelievers toward belief in Jesus. Paul's words reminded the church that society would not judge them by their theology but by their behavior. The conduct of the Thessalonian church during those tumultuous times had the potential to either glorify God or misrepresent Him to the rest of the world.

While those verses were specifically penned for a group of first-century Christians, they hold true today. We, too, can magnify or malign God to the watching world by how we respond to our circumstances. Whenever you and I feel buried with burdens, minding our own business and working with our hands can become just the shovel we need to dig our way out. Furthermore, when we make it our ambition to do both, we will not only experience the peace and rest we crave, but we'll more accurately display the gospel to others.

The Choice Is Yours

Make it your ambition—I read and reread that phrase until my eyes crossed. Those four small words declared two big things. The first was this: A quiet life was not a certainty. Paul was not providing a surefire solution. His words were a principle, not a promise. By heeding his advice, I would have a better chance of claiming peace and rest than if I just ignored his counsel. Obedience would put the odds in my favor. And the second: *Make* is a verb. My ambition or desire for a quiet life would require action. And not just any action, *my* action.

Admittedly, there will always be situations that, in my finite power, I cannot mind. No amount of work on my part will change the outcome. For instance, I will never have control over the budgeting decisions made by my husband's clients. I cannot delay the rapid decline of my mother's memory. Cancer will never be cured in my hands. And if statistics are to be trusted, deer will continue to kamikaze themselves in front of oncoming traffic during mating season. No car can ever gain immunity, including my own.

Possibly as you read this, you're replaying the last few days, months, or even years and discovering that so much of your life has felt like a hostage situation. Maybe you, too, have struggled under the weight of many outside-of-your-control circumstances, all of which have made your every day feel harder than it needs to be.

Perhaps Paul understood that everyday burden, and it was the very reason he gave his "mind your own business" proclamation. At first blush, *minding* your own business urges you to keep doing the work at hand, to train your appetites to follow through, finish a job, and stay the course. Like an athlete who aims to win, *minding* your own business requires you to remain consistent and faithful. It's often uncomfortable and, at times, necessitates self-denial. But it ensures that your responsibilities are taken care of.

Upon closer examination and with a slightly different emphasis, however, minding *your* own business implores you to keep your eyes on your own paper. It helps you to champion the work others are doing while not allowing their successes to discourage or distract you, heaping more and more on your plate.

In addition, minding your *own* business forces you to accept that some things are out of your control and not yours to mind. It urges you to relinquish seasons of deep sorrow and strife to God, trusting that in His hands and through His compassionate care, you will not be consumed (Lam. 3:22 NIV). Minding your *own* business helps you to hold your days more tenderly, treat yourself with consideration, and accept the generous support of others, knowing you don't have to hold up the entire world.

While you and I may not be able to mind certain specific devastating situations, we can mind many ordinary areas of our lives, thereby lessening the collateral damage that acute moments of disaster can bring to our days. Though some circumstances are truly overwhelming, at times being overwhelmed can be a choice. Each crazy moment of chaos will demand that you decide: *Will I give in to the cultural pressure of perfection, taking on too much in an effort to earn the praise of others? Will I attempt to carry a burden that was never mine to carry? Or will I give it all to God, set my eyes on Jesus, and do the hard work of tying all the loose ends that He's given me to tie?*

> **Minding your own business helps you to hold your days more tenderly, treat yourself with mercy, and accept the generous support of others, knowing you don't have to hold up the entire world.**

Framing *overwhelm* as a decision might appear too legalistic or pressure-filled. But let's not be guilty of crying "legalism" when what we really mean is "I'm comfortable," "Change takes work," or "I don't want to admit that some of my overwhelm is self-inflicted." In clinging to, validating, or making excuses for why we are not minding *our* business, we will never be able to step out of the mess.

What to Expect

At the risk of looking like the mustache-twirling villain in my own book, I will share with you a simple truth: If God, through Paul, called believers to the quiet life, it is because even when all the world begins to totter, peace and rest *are* possible.

This is the part of our journey together where you probably expect me to say something like, "We've all been given the same twenty-four hours in the day." But while that may be true in principle, it's grossly inaccurate in practice. So I'm not going to say it. You see, there's a big difference between the time constraints of a single, unmarried woman and those of a single mother of three. There's also quite a disparity between that same single mom's day and that of a mother who has a dependable spouse to help carry the parental load. The truth is, although we may all have twenty-four hours at our disposal, the hours aren't all the same.

I don't know which camp you fall into, nor why you decided to pick up this book. I can only assume that the word *overwhelmed* caught your attention. Perhaps you've been spinning so many plates your life looks like a low-budget circus sideshow. Or maybe your overwhelm has nurtured seeds of apathy. There are not enough hours in the day to keep up with all that your life demands and you've convinced yourself that if you can't do it all, then you might as well not even try to do any of it. It could be, instead, that your overwhelm has bred feelings of disappointment and guilt as you look around and see other women thriving while juggling twice the number of responsibilities that you have. Clearly, everyone has learned some hidden secret except you—or at least that's what you've begun to believe.

Regardless of what pulled you to these pages, I can only assume that, like the Jamie of 2022, you're not only looking for ways to reshuffle the deck—to balance what feels off-kilter—but you also want to be seen. You want someone, anyone, to notice how hard life is right now and to acknowledge that, despite being dealt blow after blow, you're still standing. You haven't given up, and *that* in itself is a victory.

Well, overwhelmed mom, I see you.

I see you, preschool wrangler, who doesn't remember what it feels like to go to the bathroom without an audience. Your toddler acts like a terrorist at every meal, threatening anarchy if you dare to give him even one more vegetable. Each day feels more tedious than the last. You feel beaten by *busy* but have nothing to show for your efforts.

I see you, mom of grade schoolers, who's busy playing chauffeur, nursemaid, head chef, laundress, and referee. Your time and patience have been stretched so thin they're both practically see-through. You're filling out permission slips, tripping over misplaced musical instruments, and navigating complicated carpool politics that make every day feel like a competition.

I see you, mature middle-ager. Your life is crowded. You still have kids at home, are launching adult children, and are helping care for aging parents. Your body is starting to betray you, so even simple tasks feel hard to do. (I don't know about you, but I blame gluten. Or maybe Big Pharma? Red dye 40?) Your marriage is well-worn. At times, that means it fits like a favorite college sweatshirt. At other times, it feels threadbare.

I see you. I won't pretend to know just how many holes are in the bottom of your leaky boat right now, but I've watched you bail water by the bucketful and row with all your might. I know you're watching the horizon, bracing for another cloud that will surely unzip a downpour, threatening shipwreck. I hope these pages will be like a life raft to pull you to the safety of shallow waters.

My words may tug on your heart in some painful ways. At times, they'll feel about as soothing as a political debate during an election year. But trust me, fragility and offense will only sabotage our time together.

I won't boss you around or guilt-monger you into doing things my way. (Social media has probably done enough of that to you already.) Besides, bookstore shelves are buckling under the weight of time management books with Take-Back-Your-Life anthems. Those messages have been delivered before. It's highly plausible you've already read many of them, yet here you are. Frankly, if you're hoping for another book that will be like all of those—a secular rosary to keep the pressures of life at bay—you should keep browsing. This is not your book.

If you're looking for a title that will encourage you just to duck out, burn everything to the ground, and start again, save your money. This is not your book. Spoiler alert: A simple do-over will lead you to the exact same pile of overwhelm if you never plan a new route along the way.

But if you're looking for a resource focusing more on biblical principles than prescriptive solutions, keep reading. These pages were written especially for you.

I know from experience that minding your own business is long-haul work. I also know you'll be more persistent in your efforts when you see small changes happen immediately. So, at the end of each chapter, I've added some thoughtful questions to help you examine how you are or are not using your time, talent, and resources in helpful ways. In addition, between every few chapters, I've included some battle-proven suggestions to help you start tackling the mother lode of Motherload you face daily. Consider these a buffet of ideas to pick and choose from.

Please know that, like Rome, order cannot be built in a day. It's taken me more than two decades of mothering and managing a household to incorporate these hacks into my home. With that in mind, don't try implementing all these tactics right this second. Doing so will only add more weight to your already heavy days. Through our time together, you'll learn to embrace what matters, shake off what doesn't, and mind your own business. Undergirded with Scripture, you'll establish some new habits, and in doing so, you'll reduce the friction you're feeling.

Together, we'll begin a revolution of peace. As Paul charges, we're going to make it our ambition to work with our hands, and we're going to do it in the unassuming corners of our everyday lives. We're going to swim against the cultural current of busy, striving for stability for ourselves and for our families. We won't be flashy, but we will be faithful.

The *quiet* starts now.

2

Narrate a Good Story

Hard is not the same thing as bad.
ABBIE HALBERSTADT

I saw a meme on social media the other day that initially made me chuckle. It was dripping with sarcasm and echoed the sentiments of so many moms. It said something like, "Adulting: 1 star. Overrated. I do not recommend." While there was a part of me that wanted to whisper, "No kidding. Where is the return policy on adult life?" I knew that this kind of viral scorn had become an online virus, infecting the hearts of women with the disease of discontent. Not surprisingly, it only took a moment for that meme to unleash a wave of jeers and sneers in the comments section of the post. Misery loves company.

"I have three kids. I didn't get an epidural at any of their births, but I'd like one now," one woman said.

"To keep my house clean, I've asked my family to go live elsewhere," said another.

Reply after reply echoed the self-diagnosed grievances of mothers all across the country, perhaps even the world. "Where's the unsubscribe button on parenting?" they all seemed to say.

No doubt looking for permission to despair, women unloaded their frustrations about life and received both validation and vitriol for their efforts. Some moms came for a fight, not a conversation. The internet is nothing if not a Petri dish of derision, I suppose. Then again, you'll find similar protests peddled offline too—on T-shirts, quote-a-day calendars, and those tiny vinyl decals conveniently placed right by the register in every North American gas station. Distress dumpings are everywhere. Clearly, when moms are unhappy, we want everyone to know about it.

Could our complaints be exacerbating the disorder that is already present?

There seems to be no end to the life-is-hard, adulting-is-hard, everything-is-just-so-hard mantras our culture has embraced. *Motherhood is miserable. So drink up. It's wine o'clock somewhere. Hide in the bathroom. Eat all the chocolate. Buy all the things. You've earned it.*

At first pass, these memes seem funny and trivial. They're laced with the kind of satire intended to make us all laugh so hard at our struggles that we can't possibly cry. Perpetuating an unhealthy form of solidarity, women share and reshare them in hopes of gathering allies. *Your life is a giant dumpster fire? Mine too! Wanna chat about it? Come on in, the water's warm.* But is it possible that all our joking is making our feelings of overwhelm worse? Granted, our grumblings aren't necessarily the cause of our chaos, but could our complaints be exacerbating the disorder that is already present?

Belief Determines Behavior

How we name our everyday circumstances matters more than we often realize. So many of our negative feelings about our lives come from how we narrate our stories to ourselves and to others. Unfortunately, bad thoughts about our work can have long taproots. If left unchecked, they can squeeze their way into our actions. Our beliefs will always determine our behaviors.

More exactly, when we view our home work as a four-letter word, we begin to treat it as such. We do it begrudgingly, if at all. Most psychologists would call this confirmation bias—the idea that if you *believe* a task will be hard, it will be. Proverbs 18:21 spins it this way, "Death and life are in the power of the tongue." What you say about yourself, your roles, and your circumstances matters. Saying you're a hot mess, even in jest, can change the entire course of your day and cause it to derail even before it has begun.

So try asking yourself this: How am I training myself to behave? What kind of day do I practice having? Who do I prepare to be by what I say about myself and my responsibilities?

The same can be said for how we talk about our husbands and kids during a difficult season. *Overwhelm* can easily lead to a victim mindset. When my day begins spinning out of control, I can take what I perceive as the less-than-stellar effort of everyone else in my home as a personal affront to me and begin spewing the poisons of shame and blame. But I am not a casualty of motherhood. My contentedness starts with me and is not contingent on outside circumstances. My family is not robbing me of purpose. Neither is yours.

> **My contentedness starts with me and is not contingent on outside circumstances. My family is not robbing me of purpose. Neither is yours.**

As women, we are the conductors of order in our homes. We set the tone. So, when things get off-balance, we have to look inward before we start pointing fingers outward. Yes, our roles as women can be difficult, but as Jeremiah 17:9 reminds us, our hearts are wicked. Our feelings can't always be trusted. And dare I say it, regardless of what time of the month it happens to be, our hormones are not an excuse to be horrendous to others.

God created emotions, even disappointment, hurt, and anger. So we don't need to feel bad for feeling. But we also don't need to let our emotions control us. Instead, we can see them as symptoms that reveal the soul-level work that still needs to be done in and through us. Before you allow a spirit of bitterness toward your husband or children to worm its way into your heart, confess any frustration or disappointment you might be carrying because of your overwhelm.

According to 1 Corinthians 13, even in troubling times, the emotion that should lead us is love—*agape* love. This is the same kind of fatherly love God lavishes on us—love that is pure and sacrificial. It's the kind of love that desires the greatest good for another regardless of what is received in return. In life, we will always go where we gaze. If we don't intentionally turn toward love, we'll keep missing it. And if we only focus on the overwhelm, we will continue to find it.

So instead of allowing the mental and emotional baggage of a typical mother lode to blind us to the goodness of what is right in front of us, let's be women who love our children more than we dislike the inconveniences of parenting them. They are not an occupational hazard.

What makes the past ten or so years so unique isn't the number of responsibilities women now have compared to past generations. One quick glance at history shows we live in a pretty cushioned culture. (I, for one, appreciate the fact that I don't have to shear the sheep, card the wool, spin the yarn, and knit by candlelight before pulling on a fall sweater.) What makes this current moment different isn't our busyness. It's that no other generation of women before us has felt the need nor has had an outlet for showcasing their lives to everyone else in such unrestricted ways. We live in a hyper-visible world. We're over-sharers who vacillate from online humble brags to "sadfishing" at lightning speed. But at what cost?

Your kids may never see that meme you shared about how they make you want to hide in the closet and eat your feelings. It's entirely possible they won't watch that caustic video you "liked" about selling one of them on eBay to collect a little spending cash. They might never know you wrote a lengthy diatribe about their childish behavior on Facebook for all to see. But one day, they *might*. Then the joke won't be quite so funny.

We live in a hyper-visible world.

Before you vent on social media, ask yourself: Would I want to go online and see the same comment or picture posted about me? Would I want my mom, neighbor, or friend to tell the world that they have to stash chocolate and booze around the house just to survive our relationship? That they can't wait for the school year to start again so they'll finally be able to pass me off to someone else for most of my waking hours?

Would I post these same words about my kids when they are old enough to be on social media and able to read them in real time? If the answer to any of these questions is no, remember Matthew 7:12, which says, "So whatever you wish that others would do to you, do also to them, for this is the Law and the Prophets." Treat others as you want to be treated, even your children—especially your children. Gossip is gossip, even if there's an element of truth to it and it is shared in jest.

Your motives make all the difference. Why do you want to post that negative comment anyway? Do you want to garner a "like" or a "me too"? Are you seeking confirmation of or permission to feel how you're feeling? Will your difficult child, difficult husband, or difficult circumstance be remedied by airing your grievances online? When it feels like an atom bomb just went off in your life, can any of your old high school friends or the moms on your child's soccer team change that? Remember, you're allowed to process your overwhelm without making a public statement about it.

If we're being completely honest with ourselves, we'd have to admit that much of our frustration about our husbands, kids, and homes stems from our constant need to compare our lives to others. We look to the curated images we see on social media and begin shoving the "ideal" of those highlight reels into the "regular" we're coping with at home, hoping they will fit. Trouble is, the two competing pictures rarely match, and we're left feeling defeated.

While that one Instagrammer's child is off rescuing trapped kittens from treetops or calmly reading books to neglected orphans, our little cherub is drinking straight from the milk carton while also attempting to launch himself down the stairs in a laundry basket wearing only a bike helmet. He's so high-octane all the time that he makes energy drinks want to drink energy drinks just to keep up with him. We secretly wonder why our kid can't be more like those other kids. Comparison then leads to complaining.

We can grow critical of others in their successes and become doubtful of ourselves and God's ability to sustain us in the work He's given. We might take to the internet to lament our lot in life and to discredit anyone who appears to have some piece of motherhood figured out. We declare that those put-together women are just too much. They're *too* put together. They're too out of touch with the rest of the pack.

Instead of seeing them as capable or conscientious, we label certain moms *fake* or *overachievers* or *legalistic Alpha Moms,* and we inadvertently convince them to diminish or hide their success to fit in. But can we just stop it with the mom-shaming already? Can we finally put an end to the judgment of all those in-control women? We all let our kids watch too much TV, forget to serve a veggie with lunch from time to time, and opt for fruit snacks on occasion instead of serving real fruit. Even those "other" moms.

Perhaps we can begin to recognize that a mother who is more gifted or able than we are in one area or another might have a few things to teach us! If we are asking God for wisdom to grow our lives, as we should be, then we shouldn't be too surprised when we become surrounded by women who are striving for excellence in some areas of their lives. Maybe they are not intimidating; maybe we are just intimidated. The two are not the same thing. Our assumption that other women are quietly criticizing us and our self-diagnosed failures is actually its own, slightly different form of legalism.

Be careful not to let your insecurities lead to cynicism. Another woman's triumph is not a threat to you. God hasn't given someone else the gift that He has for you. That means that you can sincerely celebrate the successes of a friend without negating your own successes. Conversely, it also means that you no longer have to apologize for or feel guilty about a blessing in your own life because you understand Who deserves all the credit: God, the Giver of all good gifts.

In Matthew 6:1, Jesus taught, "Beware of practicing your righteousness before other people in order to be seen by them." This might seem like a disconnect with the teaching that comes just before that, in Matthew 5:16, when Jesus said, "Let your light shine before others, so that they may see your good works and give glory to your Father who is in heaven." In both scenarios, someone is displaying their victories. The only difference between the two is the Person deserving the praise.

Marvel at the Mundane

While an impetuous online comment about not ever being able to sleep past five a.m. or having to make your coffee so strong you could cut concrete with it might be dripping with truth, it can easily lure you to defeatism by making small irritants feel torturous. Additionally, complaints about motherhood can create deep wounds for women you know whose arms are aching for a child of their own to hold. Worse yet, they offhandedly reveal your restless discontent about the work God has given you to do. Though everyone stumbles into complaining at times, unfettered grumbling is a fist of rebellion raised high against the One who has orchestrated your days. It's slanderous ingratitude that assaults God's sovereignty and His lordship.

Whether we like it or not, God, through His messenger Paul, makes it clear in Titus 2 that the most important work of a woman takes place in her home. When urging the older women to pass along sound doctrine to their younger sisters in the faith, the apostle writes, "They are to teach what is good, and so train the young women to love their husbands and children, to be self-controlled, pure, working at home, kind, submissive to their own husbands, that the word of God may not be reviled" (Titus 2:3–5).

In calling women to work at home, God is not implying that we can't work outside the home but that all of our other commitments should not come at a cost to our homes. With the exception of our worship of and obedience to Him, our work at home should be the most important to us. Everything else is a secondary calling.

To be clear, this Titus 2 mandate doesn't let men off the hook. When you back up a few verses, you see that husbands and fathers carry great responsibilities at home too. But we're not talking about them; we're talking about us. You and I will not be held accountable for someone else's obedience. God's Word doesn't suddenly become void just because our husbands may or may not follow it.

The world often assumes that when a woman serves her family and chooses to make them her most significant investment, she's doing so from a root of guilt, coercion, or ignorance. In doing so, they undervalue the home. Admittedly, it's easy to see how the "out there" work can look more important than the "right here" work. The ministry of motherhood often feels mundane and meaningless. Dispensing daily vitamins, replacing the toilet paper roll, refilling the saltshaker, adding "diapers" to the weekly shopping list—there's a reason that success in these areas never seems to make it into the family's annual Christmas letter. These are not glory jobs; they are the humble work of service. Although your husband and kids can and may do these routine tasks regularly, chances are, the daily duties of keeping the home running smoothly often fall to you.

Rest assured, Christ can empathize with a life lived in obscurity. He spent his first thirty years serving God in mundane ways. He was a carpenter whose physical work became spiritually sanctifying. Everything about His daily routine was holy because He did it faithfully for His Father. Those sowing years prepared Him for the harvest years to come.

Even after stepping into public ministry, no job was meaningless for Jesus. In the middle of a lavish wedding feast, He slipped away from the celebration to do kitchen work. When cultural custom demanded that someone wash the dung-covered feet of the weary-worn travelers, Jesus knelt down and started scrubbing. Rarely did He ever receive a "thank you" or an "attaboy" for a job well done. In fact, Luke 17:11–19 tells us that after Jesus healed ten lepers—men who had been marginalized and cast out by the rest of society and who were now fully restored by His transforming work—only one returned to voice his gratitude.

As followers of Christ, we set out to model His selfless service even when our sacrifices are never seen, appreciated, or reciprocated. His example can compel us to see the unremarkable parts of our days as an opportunity to show love in action to those God has placed in our lives. As Mother Teresa of Calcutta is believed to have said, we should "wash the plate not because it is dirty, nor because [we] were told to wash it, but because [we] love the person who will use it next." Whether caring for our families, volunteering for our communities, or plugging away at an income-producing job, every time we faithfully do the tasks set before us, as 1 Thessalonians 4 says, we bear the image of Christ to others.

> **Every time we faithfully do the tasks set before us, we bear the image of Christ to others.**

In that way, our behavior will speak a louder theology than our words. Meaning, we aren't called to dedicate our lives to working at home so that we can have exceptional marriages and well-behaved kids, although those are sometimes the natural byproducts of our commitment to our homes. We're called to the monotonous tasks of motherhood so that the world might see a striking difference in how we respond to the responsibilities we've been given. Through our work, we can push back on the effects of brokenness, helping to restore beauty and goodness to the world. This begs the question: When your friends and neighbors hear you complaining about your overwhelm—when they hear the same mournful song from you that they hear from everyone else—what might they be led to assume about your work and the One you are working for?

We can't always control our circumstances, but we can seek to control how we react to them. We can control the attention we give to difficult situations. We can control how we name them.

Renew Your Mind

Learning to change your responses will obviously take some premeditated effort, especially in a culture that champions mediocre mothering. If you've been swallowing a dose of "woe is me" with your morning coffee each day, you'll need to ready yourself for the difficult detox ahead. The good news is that your brain can be retrained. You don't have to give negative attitudes and actions more oxygen.

Since as early as the 1960s, scientists have known that neurons and neural networks in the brain have the ability to change their typical behavior in response to certain factors like new information, aging, or trauma.[1] Psychiatrists use this neuroplasticity, as it is called, to help people with PTSD, severe depression, and anxiety to begin reframing unhealthy thought patterns to heal.

We can't always control our circumstances, but we can seek to control how we react to them.

Just as a rut was created through the soft, impressionable soil of the prairie grasses every time a wagon passed over it on its way westward, creating a "road" for future pioneers to travel with ease, your thought life creates highways in your brain. Each time you respond to the difficulties of motherhood with criticism, lament, or hostility, the negativity digs a deeper and deeper groove in your neural networks. Eventually, the "track" becomes so fixed and well-worn that you get stuck in the rut, involuntarily controlled by instinct.

So our lives become shaped by what we persistently think about and how we think about those things. The *feeling* of failure often rises up well before failure actually happens. These negative thoughts can seal the deal by convincing us to give up. Inversely, the good news is that feelings of success can predict victory. By learning correct responses to certain triggers and practicing coping strategies, we can not only reroute our reactions before they become permanent fixtures in our motherhood but also rewire our brains to shape our world differently.[2] Science calls this process of laying down new neural ruts cognitive behavioral therapy. Romans 12:2 calls it "the renewal of your mind."

If you're in Christ, you're instructed to put off the old attitudes of dissension, cynicism, and resentment and put on the fruit of the Spirit—love, joy, peace, patience, kindness, goodness, faithfulness, gentleness, and self-control (Gal. 5:22–23).

While God, through His Spirit, will do much of that renewal by directing your thoughts toward the truth and illuminating your understanding of certain encouraging Scriptures, He welcomes you into the supernatural work. Begin today to lay down fresh tracks where deep furrows once forced your responses in unhelpful directions.

Recognize that the defeatist thoughts come from the enemy. Satan wants you to live in the places that you cannot change—the past and the future. As the father of lies, his primary aim is always to get you to doubt the goodness of God. He'll wield the two-edged sword of regret and fear to convince you to loathe even the loveliest parts of your life.

But God has you right here, right now. When you learn to narrate a good story about your current situation, you also learn to handle your busyness differently. At the first sign of overwhelm, you don't blame shift, lose your cool on your husband or children, or take to the internet to declare you've been handed a raw deal. Instead, you begin to bring your struggles to God in prayer. When push comes to shove, the internet might give you sympathy, but what you really need is supernatural strength.

God has you right here, right now.

Ask the Lord to guide and guard your thoughts about your current situation. May your first knee-jerk reaction in the face of overwhelm soon become a desire to drop to your knees. Some would see prayer as a last resort or a posture of defeat, but when you're navigating many land mines in your day, prayer should be your first line of defense. Prayer is an acknowledgment of your dependence upon God. It is a deliberate admission that the burdens of this world are too heavy for you to bear and a recognition that He alone upholds all of creation.

God's power cannot only help you tackle the tasks at hand, but it can also bring dead things to life. It can resurrect your feelings about your home, your children, and the work He's given you to do. Call upon God to temper your responses with gentleness and generosity of spirit. Pray that He removes any growing irritation and allows you to see the mundane liturgies of scrubbing faces, chopping veggies, or returning misplaced items to their rightful places as an opportunity for worship. Ask that you'd begin to see service within your home as sanctifying work—a holy labor that will birth a more Christlike you.

Lately, my personal prayer has been, "Lord, make me a woman who is controlled by your Spirit and not my own selfish ambitions or vain flesh (Rom. 8:12–14). Guard my heart and my mind against any thought that would cause me to doubt or disobey you (Phil. 4:7). When I'm tempted to flavor my words with anger or sarcasm, close my mouth. But give me the boldness to open it and share your love with others (Prov. 17:27–28). Help me to be purposeful with my time, self-controlled with my emotions, and diligent in the responsibilities you've given me today (Col. 3:23). May I be content with what I have (Phil. 4:11–13). When I'm faced with hard things and pressed on all sides, help me respond in faith and not fear (Ps. 56:3–4). Give me the discernment needed to tackle today and the courage to place tomorrow's troubles in your hands (Prov. 3:5–6). May my hope be found only in You (Rom. 15:13). I'm not asking for a different set of circumstances, God. I'm asking that Your Son be seen in me no matter my circumstances. Amen."[3]

Put in the right words so that the right words will come out. Begin hiding God's Word in your heart by memorizing Scripture that pertains to your particular struggle and the negative responses you're prone to give to it. Write the verses out on sticky notes and place them strategically around your home where you'll see them most often—the bathroom mirror, the refrigerator door, or the screen saver of your phone. What you put in your mind becomes your mindset. God's Word can not only provide practical wisdom for your stressful situation, but it can strengthen your daily faith in God by reminding you who He is, what He has done, and what He promises to do on behalf of you and your kids. When you meditate on Scripture, you turn the focus away from yourself and your struggles and place it on the One who is mighty to save. Your worry then turns to worship. You can take whatever is currently plaguing your heart and offer it up as a prayer.

Recall and rehearse what you know to be true about God. The Lord is intimately acquainted with the struggles of this life. Your overwhelm has not taken Him by surprise. Your need is not a burden to Him. He sees you (Ps. 32:8). He hears every desperate cry that falls from your lips (Ps. 120:1). So seek the Lord with boldness, knowing that when and if you fall back into old tracks of blame and shame, He can provide new beginnings (Lam. 3:22–23). He can help you carve better ruts.

> **When you meditate on Scripture, you turn the focus away from yourself and your struggles and place it on the One who is mighty to save.**

Motherhood is hard, making it all too easy to perpetuate the idea of adult abdication. But children are not problems to fix, and they're not sand in the gears. According to Psalm 127:3, they are gifts—even yours. Will they do anything today, next week, or next month that will rub you the wrong way, make more work for you, or cause a wrinkle in your well-laid plans? Probably! But Jesus never promised an easy life. Acknowledging that up front will help you be a gatekeeper of your feelings and put your overwhelming circumstances in their proper place.

Does that mean you can never talk to friends about your struggles, that you can't ask for advice or encouragement from others about your current situation? Absolutely not. There is an appropriate time and place to express your feelings of overwhelm. God has placed certain people in your boat to help you navigate rough waters. We'll discuss healthy venting more in chapter 8.

For now, do yourself a favor: Ignore the "hot mess" messages of our culture, stop throwing stones at your family so your hands are free enough to wash their feet, and begin to lay new thought tracks about the work God has given you to do. Narrate a good story about your overwhelming circumstances, and you'll find that you'll grow into that story through habitual retelling.

Things to Ponder

While taking time out to think through these questions might feel like one more task to add to your Motherload, I hope you'll find that your sacrifice is time well spent—and ultimately that your answers will help you overcome your overwhelm.

1. What circumstances are causing the most overwhelm in your life right now?
2. Name the specific emotions you are currently feeling because of the overwhelming situation.
3. If belief determines behavior, what kind of day do you practice having based on what you say about the tasks ahead?
4. In the past, what coping strategies have you employed for overwhelming circumstances? Have these methods been successful in helping you calm the chaos?

> **5.** Seek out three to five verses in Scripture that might help move your gaze from your struggles to the Savior who overcomes them (maybe even from the suggested Scriptures in this chapter). Write them down and place them strategically in your home, where you'll see them often.
>
> **6.** Take a few moments to pray about the specific struggles you listed above, asking God for the wisdom to know how best to tackle them, the strength to do the required work, and the self-control to not get distracted or become discontent along the way.

Wisdom from God's Word

Philippians 2:1–11
Philippians 4:4–8
James 3:3–18

The Motherload: Prayer Life

Overwhelm in certain areas of motherhood can grow and magnify feelings of loneliness, despondency, and anxiety. Memorizing and meditating on the Scriptures can help you form new thought tracks about your current responsibilities. The following is a list of verses to help you reframe your current situation:

Colossians 3:23–24

"Whatever you do, work heartily, as for the Lord and not for men, knowing that from the Lord you will receive the inheritance as your reward. You are serving the Lord Christ."

Whether you're wiping a baby's bottom or leading a boardroom full of suits, you are doing it unto the Lord. All your work has purpose and requires your mindfulness, dedication, and creativity.

Proverbs 14:1

"The wisest of women builds her house, but folly with her own hands tears it down."

The way you talk about your husband and children can either make your home a holy habitation or a pit of destruction for you and for them.

Philippians 2:3–4

"Do nothing from selfish ambition or conceit, but in humility count others more significant than yourselves. Let each of you look not only to his own interests, but also to the interests of others."

You are an emissary of God's love to your family. That love leaves no room for bitterness, pride, or malicious comments, whether online or in person. Preschoolers who still wet the bed, middle schoolers who forget their science homework on the school bus, college students who bring a semester's worth of dirty clothes home with them at Thanksgiving break—they aren't interruptions to your life; they are your life.

Psalm 32:8

"I will instruct you and teach you in the way you should go; I will counsel you with my eye upon you."

Home is the place where your kids can grow more hardworking, more dependable, more kind, and more Christlike. But home is also the place where *you'll* grow more too. God sees your busyness.

Moreover, He is willing and able to help you find a way forward and to help you grow into the work at hand.

Psalm 120:1

"In my distress I called to the Lord, and he answered me."

As He did with young David who penned these words while his enemy slandered his work, God stands ready to defend your mothering against any shame or apathy the accuser hurls your way.

Hebrews 4:15–16

"For we do not have a high priest who is unable to sympathize with our weaknesses, but one who in every respect has been tempted as we are, yet without sin. Let us then with confidence draw near to the throne of grace, that we may receive mercy and find grace to help in time of need."

Our Lord has worn the flesh of humanity, experiencing similar struggles to your own. Your need is not a burden to Him; He wants to help. So seek Him with boldness.

Lamentations 3:22–23

"The steadfast love the Lord never ceases; his mercies never come to an end; they are new every morning; great is your faithfulness."

If you feel like a less-than mother today, take comfort in knowing God provides new beginnings every morning. He's not a God of "I told you so" or "I thought you knew better." He's a God of do-overs and second chances.

1 John 5:14–15

"And this is the confidence that we have toward him, that if we ask anything according to his will he hears us. And if we know that he hears us in whatever we ask, we know that we have the requests that we have asked of him."

You may never have an opportunity to have certain conversations with others about your sensitive circumstances. But you can always have these discussions with God. He may not remove the struggles in your life, but He will surely uphold you as you face them.

Philippians 4:4–7

"Rejoice in the Lord always; again I will say, rejoice. Let your reasonableness be known to everyone. The Lord is at hand; do not be anxious about anything, but in everything by prayer and supplication with thanksgiving let your requests be made known to God. And the peace of God, which surpasses all understanding, will guard your hearts and your minds in Christ Jesus."

As you encounter struggles this week—disappointments, unkind people, and trials of all kinds—remember that you're facing them with the power of the Holy Spirit. Allow your daily interactions and reactions to display God's true character. Ask Him to help you respond in ways that reveal His light to the world.

Galatians 6:9–10

"And let us not grow weary of doing good, for in due season we will reap, if we do not give up. So then, as we have opportunity, let us do good to everyone, and especially to those who are of the household of faith."

Jesus never promised an easy life, so don't walk away from Him just because things have gotten difficult. Don't allow seeds of discontent to grow. Keep on weeding them out. Remain faithful to the work He has given you, trusting that your efforts will reap a harvest that can last for generations.

3

Edit with Intention

If we really have too much to do, there are some items on the agenda that God did not put there. Let us submit the list to Him and ask Him to indicate which items we must delete. There is always time to do the will of God. If we are too busy to do that, we are too busy.
ELISABETH ELLIOT

The year was 2010. I was in the shallow end of my thirties, happily married to my college sweetheart, and stockpiling diaper coupons like I was preparing for the apocalypse. Prince William was stirring up a media frenzy after finally popping the question to his longtime girlfriend, Kate Middleton. The paparazzi couldn't get enough of the power couple. Lady Gaga was also creating quite a bit of buzz on the red carpet, not for her song lyrics but for showcasing over-the-top fashion choices. (You can't unsee a dress made entirely of meat, folks.) And a group of Angry Birds had captured the attention of nearly every American middle schooler.

Distracted by these and other "trending" topics, the world never noticed when three relatively unknown web developers slipped in the back door of the internet and rolled out the invitation-only Beta version of Pinterest. This new social media platform would help define the entire decade. And yet, even today, you'd be hard-pressed to find any news stories about the website written in the first year of its inception. It was a sleeper hit that online moguls and investors just didn't see coming.

Perhaps that's because its immediate success was slow-going. Instead of pouring money into glossy publicity campaigns, its makers relied on grassroots, word-of-mouth advertising. And their efforts, or lack thereof, paid off. Analysts report that Pinterest "was the fastest site in history to reach 10 million unique monthly visitors."[1] Eventually, over 80 percent of mothers in the US who used the internet were at least casual visitors of the platform.[2] They were "pinning" on their lunch breaks, in the afterschool pickup line, and while they brushed their teeth before falling into bed each night.

Hoping to overhaul their lives with quick-fix solutions, moms surrendered "good" and reached for "best" instead. Like Eve staring at the tree that promised a better life, a more important life, an enlightened life, women succumbed to the low-hanging fruit of overemphasized superlatives. Clickbait titles like "Top 3 Tips for Growing Better Succulents," "5 Sure-Fire Ways to Transform a Mom Bod by Summer," and "The Best Recipes for Soup Season" lured so many of us to read and pin lest we miss out on some important something.

We pinned, liked, and hearted. We wanted to stand out in our personal real-life circles not for being different but for being the same with excellence. Somehow, though, even after plunking down real cash money for that must-have spiralizer and following the directions for all thirty of the exceptionally complicated "Easy Zucchini Spaghetti" recipes we pinned to our "What's Cooking" board, our children still turned up their noses at dinner time.

If memory serves, thanks to my itchy pinning finger, that was the year

I made my first quilt. It was supposed to be a lap-style blanket to match my living room, but because of my poor red and green color selections, it was permanently exiled to the Christmas bin. I took up canning that year too. In hindsight, I'm confident the toddler puking incident of 2011 can be pinned, quite literally, on an improperly sealed jar of peaches. And who can forget the Amish Friendship Bread that hijacked an entire section of coveted counter space in my kitchen? Feeding, weighing, and discarding remnants of gelatinous dough became my part-time job.

My pins and boards quickly created the best version of me, the Patron Saint of Productivity, or so I thought. To be fair, Pinterest wasn't the only online influence in my life or in the lives of my friends. Fellow 2010 social media alums Instagram and Snapchat, as well as the founding members of the social elite, Twitter (later renamed X) and Facebook, were also changing the way many moms spent their time. They made us tilt toward new positions, pursue new passions, and hold ourselves to new standards. They slowly transformed the way we viewed each other and ourselves.

Silence Your Smartphone

Now, more than fifteen years later, none of these online platforms are the social heavyweights that they once were, but their reverberating effects are still influencing our motherhood. We feel busy and overwhelmed, but according to recent findings by Harmony Healthcare IT, most of us spend five hours and sixteen minutes a day on our smartphones.[3] To put that number into perspective, we apparently devote more than a twenty-four-hour day each week to our mobile devices. This average does not include the time we spend on other screens like televisions, computers, and tablets, but only what we squander on our phones.

Our obsession with smartphones reminds me of an infamous scene in *Gulliver's Travels*. After observing the shipwrecked sailor and taking copious notes on his behavior, the six-inch-tall Lilliputians assumed that because Gulliver kept checking his pocket watch, it must be his god. Surely anything that commands so much time and attention is worthy of worship, they deduce.[4] In a few satirical paragraphs, eighteenth-century author Jonathan Swift highlighted two key dangers of tech: it's distracting and addictive. It changes culture by changing us.

Nearly three hundred years after Swift's prophetic words, we still walk around wearing watches, but now they are smart. Like Gulliver, we spend every spare moment tapping, scrolling, and checking. On average, you and I get sixty to eighty notifications daily, with some of us reportedly getting as many as two hundred.[5] We can hop on social media and, in less than three seconds, scroll past a time-lapse video of a gender-reveal party we forgot to attend, an advertisement for a new fast-food restaurant opening in the area, an announcement about the impending divorce of a college roommate, a funny cat meme from a coworker, a political rant from the dad of a high school friend, a cousin's opinion of last night's game, an invitation to a jewelry party from another mom in our daughter's class at school, the overly intimate vacation photos from the childhood friend we just reconnected with, and the address of a multi-family garage sale hosted by the church youth group.

We were never meant to care as deeply about everything and everyone. We were not made to contend with the sheer volume of voices the internet shoves at us. The noise is too loud. The emotional weight is too heavy. Our phones and the social hysteria they cultivate leave us so emotionally depleted that we can no longer rejoice and weep with those who are standing right in front of us, breathing the same air. Social media lets us follow ten different plot lines at a time. It's too much. The continual stream of information increases our cognitive load (the amount of data we have to process daily) and leaves us with tech fatigue. We feel both mentally and physically exhausted at the push of a button. Our brains cannot keep up with the constant downloading of knowledge, and we lack the wisdom and discernment to know what to do with it all.

We naively assume a smartphone or watch will multiply our presence, allowing us to get more done in less time—but it won't. Only God is omnipresent. Persistently checking our phones actually undermines our efforts as it diminishes our productivity. Gloria Mark, professor in the Department of Informatics at the University of California, Irvine, concluded that it takes an average of twenty-three minutes and fifteen seconds to return to a task after you've been interrupted. An interruption shifts your thinking. It takes some time to tackle the interruption and then time to remember where you were at in the original task and resume working.[6] Put another way, switching activities fragments the day. Every time you or I stop what we are currently doing to send a text, check social media, or reply to an email, we are basically training our minds to be unfocused, which saps our decision-making skills and increases our anxiety and stress levels. We live in a sustained state of survival mode because we feel we just can't keep up.

> *We were not made to contend with the sheer volume of voices the internet shoves at us. The noise is too loud. The emotional weight is too heavy.*

While a phone itself is innocuous, mounting evidence suggests that how we physically respond to it may not be. Every time you or I hear the ping of a notification, our brains release a small level of dopamine, a neurotransmitter directly connected to the reward system of our bodies. Dopamine is the chemical that gets released whenever we have a pleasurable experience, like enjoying time with friends, eating a delicious meal, or having sex. It's also a key ingredient in our "flight or fight" response when we encounter a harmful situation.[7]

Normal amounts of this "feel-good hormone," as it is often called, are necessary and can improve a person's memory, attention, mood, and sleep. But, as with anything, too much of a good thing is not good. In the same way that dopamine contributes to the increased anticipation a gambling addict feels each time he pulls the lever, making him want to pull again and again in order to experience that same level of excitement, dopamine compels us to keep checking our phones. Our excessive daily amounts of "happy hits" can have harmful and lasting effects, including obesity, addiction, and escalating levels of anxiety and depression.[8]

For most phone users, myself included, the pattern of destruction is cyclical. The never-ending barrage of information thrust upon us every time we pick up our phones leaves us listless and lifeless. We have a less-than-accurate perception of time while staring at a screen and can easily fritter away large swaths of the day. These lost moments put us further behind in our to-do lists, which only exacerbates our feelings of inattention and overwhelm. Not only that, but the polarizing nature of social media can often leave us feeling disappointed, frustrated, and even enraged. We then scroll more often in order to sedate our minds. We become consumers of culture instead of producers of it.

Too much of a good thing is not good.

Research suggests that you and I check our phones within five minutes after receiving a notification. We're like lab rats trained to run toward the cheese whenever we hear a bell chime, never realizing that poison's been injected into every tiny morsel. Why is it so hard for us to set our phones aside? Are we afraid of what we'll hear in the deafening silence when our devices are turned off?

Proverbs 25:28 warns that "a man without self-control is like a city broken into and left without walls." I can't think of a better picture of how I feel when I'm overwhelmed than a city that has become vulnerable and exposed because its defensive protection has been allowed to crumble. It hasn't offensively fortified itself and, as a result, suffers some dire consequences.

We need to edit. To delete. To unsubscribe. I'm not suggesting we have a Luddite overreaction to tech. For most moms, especially those of us who work online and who cannot permanently escape the digital devils in our pockets, complete smartphone renunciation is not possible. Since we no longer live in an age of pay phones on every street corner or landlines in every home, I am grateful to have timely connectivity to my family, my friends, and a 911 operator should I ever need it. (Trust me, in a household of four active teenage boys, I sleep better at night knowing that a triage nurse is available at the touch of a screen.) What I am saying is that perhaps we'd feel less busy by taking a few precautionary measures to help protect our time and mental health.

Admittedly, my relationship with my phone has been more complicated in certain seasons of my life than in others. I'm still a work in progress. However, in the last few years, I've made a few changes to my normal cellphone routine to help create better digital boundaries. None of these are long-term solutions for the overwhelm you might feel, but they may temporarily reduce your mental clutter, prevent your phone from becoming all-consuming, and perhaps give back some much-needed time in your days.

- Turn off all phone notifications. Determine a set time(s) each day to manually check certain apps. Be proactive in your phone use, not reactive.
- Delete any unnecessary apps.
- Take a phone sabbath one day a week. Set your phone to "Do not disturb" mode. Place the numbers of your husband or children on

"emergency" so you can still be reached by them when needed. If one full day of phone rest is impossible, aim for half a day.
- Put your social media icons on your last home screen, making them more difficult to access.
- Turn your home screen to greyscale. The muted color won't be as distracting.
- Use an app like RescueTime to track your social media use and to turn off any apps after you've used them for a predetermined amount of time to prevent accidental overuse.
- Don't charge your phone in your bedroom at night so you can get a full night's sleep without the bothersome ping of notifications.
- Place your phone inside a container or an internal pocket of your purse. You'll still be able to hear and answer incoming calls and texts but will be forced to exert more effort to retrieve it for passive scrolling.
- Consider switching to a dumb phone—a traditional mobile phone or a flip phone that does not have internet access.
- Keep your schedule in an analog calendar, hand-write recipes, and create lists on scratch pads. The more you use old-fashioned pen and paper to tend to your life, the less often you'll need to reach for a phone and its distractions.

Care Less About More Things

The communication revolution has changed us in other ways too. We've grown so accustomed to listening to a chorus of bossy internet voices telling us what we "should" and "must" do that we now struggle to listen to the still, small Voice that matters most. Instead of submitting our days to the will of God and the tasks He has set before us, we succumb to the try-hard gospel, crowbarring more and more and more into our days.

In one breath, we say, "I'm so overwhelmed." Yet in the very next breath, we say, "I want to raise chickens, expand my garden, bake all my own bread, cook all our food from scratch, homeschool my children, run a successful online business, volunteer to teach Sunday school each week, organize a fundraiser, start a book club, plan a date night with my husband, run for city council, join a class at the gym, adopt a shelter dog, reduce my consumption of single-use products, make a meal for my sick neighbor, and repaint the front entry. This week." Like Eve, we fall for the lie of limitlessness.

We've grown so accustomed to listening to a chorus of bossy internet voices telling us what we "should" and "must" do that we now struggle to listen to the still, small Voice that matters most.

In her book *Unfinished Business,* former Princeton dean and president of the American Society of International Law Anne-Marie Slaughter had this to say about the illusion of an everything life: "I had always believed, and told all the young women I taught and mentored, that women could 'have it all.' They just had to be committed enough."[9] She had bought into the cultural lie that determination determines one's limitations. But after serving for a time in the US State Department doing the brain-breaking work of policy planning, Slaughter realized that "even the most organized and most competent multitasker . . . can reach her limit."[10] Recognizing how short-tempered and unhealthy she was becoming in trying to be all things to all people, she resigned from her position to devote more time to her son. She confessed that most women, herself included, tend to hold themselves to an unrealistic standard. They want to do it all and do it all right now.

It's impossible to have an everything life. Only God is everything. And while we were made to be *like* God, we were never meant to *be* God.

As an image bearer, you can create, but you are not the Creator. In our prideful attempts at perfection, we have become approval junkies with too many competing priorities. Overdose is inevitable. What will feel like overwhelm to us will look a lot like anger, frustration, and disappointment to anyone who happens to be standing close by—most likely our husband and children.

The antidote seems obvious: We need to scale back. We need to begin to care less about more things. The first step in having the life we actually want is to get rid of the life we don't. Author Greg McKeown calls this the disciplined pursuit of less, or essentialism. "Essentialism," he writes, "is not about how to get more things done; it's about how to get the right things done. It doesn't mean just doing less for the sake of less either. It is about making the wisest possible investment of your time and energy in order to operate at your highest point of contribution by doing only what is essential."[11]

We need to decide what is ours to do and then be willing to dismiss the rest. We need to say *no*, not because we are busy but because we don't want to be busy.

That word *decide* is an interesting one. It comes from two Latin roots, *de*, which means "off," and *caedere*, which means "to cut."[12] In other words, the best way to decide what matters most is to first cut off what doesn't. We have to edit with intention. We have to make a NO list.

It might seem counterintuitive to care less when your day demands so much more from you, but every farmer will tell you that if you want a quality harvest come fall, you have to be willing to thin out the crops in the spring. Thinning ensures that each plant will have adequate root space for growth. Additionally, when they are not competing for sunlight, water, and nutrients, plants will produce the choicest possible fruit. Cutting off, thinning, pruning—they all help a farmer to nurture quality, not quantity. They help him grow precisely what he wants and intends to grow. By deciding early what to thin out, he doesn't have to expel extra energy later on deciding what to keep.

In that way, a scheduling decision has less to do with choosing how you are going to spend your time and more about how you're not going to spend it. By processes of elimination, you can immediately see the difference between the good fruit and the best fruit. As a busy mom, you don't have the luxury of caring about things that don't matter to you.

> *The best way to decide what matters most is to first cut off what doesn't. We have to edit with intention. We have to make a NO list.*

Did you notice the prepositional phrase at the end of that last sentence? *To you.* Those two words may be small, but they can make a big difference in your day, week, year, and life.

What matters *to you* may or may not matter to anyone else. Conversely, what matters to someone else may carry very little importance in your life. Remember Paul's admonition from 1 Thessalonians 4:11? "You should mind your own business," he wrote. He never said to mind the business of your neighbor, your best friend, or your mother-in-law. His charge was to mind *your* business. You are in control of every *yes* and *no* you give. You, and you alone, will bear the weight of what you choose to mind. So give careful consideration to what matters *to you* lest you become a victim of someone else's convictions or lack thereof.

Case in point: I rarely fold clean socks. I don't often require my kids to fold them, either. Mostly, we gather all the freshly laundered socks and toss them all into one big basket that sits at the bottom of the linen closet. When someone needs socks, he or she rummages through the basket to find a match and puts them on. Instead of spending ten minutes twice a week reuniting perfect pairs, we each spend about thirty seconds a day grabbing what works. The end. This willy-nilly approach to footwear makes my friend Emily react like a cat with its back up. She would never think of chucking an unmatched merino wool crew-length next to a cotton athletic ankle-cut. Folded socks are important to her.

While Emily's folding socks twice a week, I'm in the kitchen chopping two or three cloves of garlic during dinner prep each evening, something she never does. She prefers to buy jars of minced garlic and plop a few spoonfuls into her simmering pot. I could drill her with all the reasons I think fresh garlic is more flavorful and maintains much higher allicin levels for preventing blood clots, cancer, and bacterial infections than the prepackaged stuff. I could give her facts, statistics, and personal testimonies to prove my point. But no amount of TED Talking would change her mind. Not even a little bit. Why? Because guilt is a horrible long-term motivator and because garlic just doesn't matter to Emily. She's already put it on her NO list.

In the same way you'll never open up one of my dresser drawers and find perfectly symmetrical rows of socks, you'll never find a bulb of raw garlic in Emily's kitchen cupboard. We both determined long ago what to edit out of our days. Chopping garlic is a NO for her; folding socks is a NO for me.

I realize that eliminating a ten-minute task from your schedule will not move the needle much, if at all. When the storms of life are raging, caring for hosiery won't be the final wave that pulls you under. But, if you were to spend ten minutes a week doing an incidental task that doesn't really matter to you, folding socks or otherwise, you'd end up donating nine whole hours of your life each year to someone else's cause. Your socks would get folded, but something else would surely be left undone, perhaps something more important to you.

The same can be said of consequential social or ecological causes you'd love to be able to honor but which seem to dominate more than their share of your mental and physical reserves during a difficult season. Avoiding one-time-use products, fast fashion, or carbon emissions out of conviction to love your neighbor and future generations well is a great goal, but if the price of doing so has you so overwhelmed you can't function, you need to set those goals aside until you can come back at them someday in health. It's impossible to save the whales while drowning, after all.

When you don't preemptively determine what you won't do, you can easily fall prey to the tyranny of the urgent. Your continued *yes* will be a solicitation for others to enlist your help, especially when they are under the gun. As followers of Christ, we are, of course, called to bear one another's burdens (Gal. 6:2). We are to love others in the same way that Christ loved us and gave Himself up for us (Eph. 5:2). We are to consider the interests of others ahead of our own (Phil. 2:4). But we also have to remember that when we're saying yes to someone, we are saying *no* to someone else. A commitment may not be right for you if it affects how you love the ones you love most or if it steals your joy so much that you have none left to give to others.

If we're not careful to set boundaries ahead of time, our busyness can become lethal to our family. Someone else's lack of planning can quickly become our emergency, and the people entrusted to our care end up with nothing but our leftovers.

So begin setting *no* goals with the same fervor and energy you give to setting *yes* goals. Ask yourself, *What do I find myself skipping or ignoring often?* The answer is a big indication of what needs to be addressed. If something has repeatedly fallen to the bottom of your pile of importance, even when that task might sit at the very tip-top of someone else's, it may be time to give it an official *no*, to edit it out with intention. It might be time to remove it from your to-dos.

I realize this advice might not sit well with some folks. Intentionally *not* matching socks may take courage. But, the truth is, if they are not getting matched anyway because you just don't have the time or energy to sort socks, erasing that task from your list of weekly chores doesn't greatly change the status quo. It merely releases you from the guilt you feel for not having folded them. If they are not on your "list," then you never have to feel like a failure for not checking them off as "done."

> **Begin setting no *goals* with the same fervor and energy you give to setting yes *goals*.**

What's Your Why?

A straightforward way to determine what responsibilities should or should not be eliminated from your days is to examine your motivation for doing them in the first place. I don't know about you, but I've longed to be longed for my entire life. Maybe it's a carry-over from my '80s childhood when rank was won and lost by how quickly you were picked to be on one Red Rover team or the other. Since I was never heavy enough to break through the human chain, no one wanted me on their side. I was a social pariah. Even before I could tie my shoes, I had already learned a crucial but misguided lesson in our Western caste system: According to the culture, my value is determined by what I do, not by who I am. I've been brainwashed into believing that my worth is found in how much weight I can carry for everyone else.

Though it's nice to feel needed, there's a difference between doing something out of love and doing something to be loved. Now, anytime I feel tattered and torn up by the opinions of others, I look to Ephesians 1:4-6 to do some necessary repair work. It reads, "He chose us in Him before the foundation of the world, that we should be holy and without blame before Him in love, having predestined us to adoption as sons by Jesus Christ to Himself, according to the good pleasure of His will, to the praise of the glory of His grace, by which He made us accepted in the Beloved" (NKJV). These verses remind me that because I'm in Christ, I'm not just acceptable, I'm fully accepted. I don't have to strain. I don't have to strive. My value and affirmation come from Him. I've already been chosen, so I have nothing to prove.

> *There's a difference between doing something out of love and doing something to be loved.*

Neither do you, friend. Be careful not to medicate your loneliness, your insecurities, and your anxieties with the placebo of busyness. In filling your schedule with a thousand different things because you fear the stillness that is sure to follow when the plates stop spinning, you're avoiding your sin sickness. You're potentially taking all the attention away from the deep soul work that needs to be done.

God is still in the business of repairing what is broken in me. While I no longer suffer from the disease to please, I still often find myself doing all the right things for all the wrong reasons. Pride is baked into my bones. When asked to lead this team of people or plan that fundraiser, I vainly believe that I alone can fulfill the need, and so it is my duty to volunteer. (Same poison. Different bottle.) *I am capable. I am able. And clearly, no one else can tackle this task*, I tell myself. Granted, I never say those words out loud, but I shout them with my actions every time I cram my calendar with yet another important something.

I don't want to disappoint. I don't want to be the reason something fails or flounders, so I sometimes agree to take on responsibilities I shouldn't. I can't slow down lest barnacles begin to grow on me. As the old saying goes, "If you want something done, ask a busy person." The more things I do, the more things I get asked to do. I am a natural *yes* girl. Since you're reading this book, I can only assume you are too.

But the truth is, sometimes saying *no* is the most loving thing you and I can do. If we don't arrogantly fill a role that is not ours to fill, we leave an empty space for someone else to fill—someone whose gifts and abilities have remained dormant for lack of use, an outlier who needs to be welcomed in, a person God wants to grow and equip for this very task. When we co-sign on a project simply because we *can* do it, forgetting to ask God if we *ought* to do it, we risk robbing someone else of being used by Him to do the work.

Last year, when the coordinator of our local soup kitchen needed more help planning and shopping for meals, she asked if I would take on the additional responsibility. I had been volunteering once a month for around four years, and as a middle-aged woman among a sea of teens and twentysomethings, I was the most experienced pair of hands in her lineup.

Sometimes saying no is the most loving thing you and I can do.

From a casual glance, it made sense that I should take on this role. I was already serving. What difference could a simple job title change possibly make? After prayerfully considering it for a few months, sweeping the corners of the potential commitment, I began to count the hidden costs of a *yes*—the little incidental tasks that aren't always obvious from the start, the brainstorming and worry work I'd inevitably carry out each month. I'd not just be taking on additional leadership responsibilities in the kitchen on the service day, but I'd also be in charge of meal planning, grocery shopping, and long-term food storage. My once-a-month volunteer role would balloon beyond my capacity, plundering not just my time but my mental energy.

Matthew 5:37 makes it clear that we are to mindfully measure every *yes* and *no* we dole out: "But let your 'Yes' be 'Yes,' and your 'No,' 'No.' For whatever is more than these is from the evil one" (NKJV). While this verse explicitly censures the use of oaths, it also holds value for daily decision-making.

I wanted to be a keeper of my word. A *yes* given out of vanity, guilt, or coercion would only end in tears and venom later when I realized I had taken on too much. That would not be loving or fair to anyone involved. So I respectfully declined, trusting that if God wanted this particular meal ministry to continue, He would provide just the right person to fill in the gaps.

Little did I know that, within a few weeks of my *no*, a retired nurse would join our team. Although she had been attending our church for almost a year, she had never really plugged into a ministry because she wasn't sure how her gifts of compassion and care might best be used. Regrettably, no one had bothered to show her.

As a seasoned mother and grandmother, this woman knew how to prepare large quantities of food on a tight budget. Additionally, her retirement afforded her ample time to focus on the kind of menu planning, bulk buying, and kitchen management that a meal center demands. I had pridefully worried that if I didn't take charge, the wheels would come off the entire thing. I feared my refusal was uncharitable. My thoughtful no turned out to be the least selfish answer I could give because it opened up room to welcome her yes.

Oftentimes, the most challenging part of creating "the good life" isn't figuring out what you care about. The hardest part will almost always be honoring what you care about enough to let the rest go. Time is the currency of life. Once a moment is spent, you can't win it back, you can't earn it back, and you can't buy it back. Anything that costs you your peace is too expensive.

Overwhelmed Mom

So here is your permission to let go of the guilt. Here is your blessing to turn down your phone and cast off the judgments of others. Here is your open door to embrace what matters most to you. If after you've thinned your schedule, planning the elaborate family photo shoot in a cornfield with complementary outfits made from ethically sourced cotton or buying bootleg milk from a local farmer each week is still standing, then by all means, gather your linen-clad kids and a handful of glass jars and head to the farm south of town. But if not, pluck them both out on purpose. Edit, edit, edit. And then edit some more.

Things to Ponder

1. If you have a smartphone, consider tracking your usage for a day. What apps command your most attention?

2. What step can you commit to today to decrease your screen time?

3. What is one area of life that continues to fall to the bottom of your pile of to-dos? Might this be something you can edit today? How can you trim back, lessen, or say *no* to this responsibility?

4. Have you ever said *yes* to a commitment when you knew you should've said *no*? Over time, how did you grow to feel about the responsibility?

5. Examine the extra commitments you have in your life—anything besides keeping home and child-rearing. Ask yourself *why* you are participating in each activity. Contemplate your answers. Are there any that feel laced with

> pride, guilt, or coercion? If so, how might you best back out of them in a loving and honoring way?

Wisdom from God's Word

Matthew 6:19–21
1 Corinthians 6:12
Titus 2:11–14

The Motherload: Decluttering

Entire industries have been created to help women overcome their overwhelm, and yet we are more anxious, worried, and dazed than ever before. Why? Because adding more clutter to a cluttered life only adds more clutter. So be careful not to throw your money at your overwhelm, assuming that if you just had the right baskets, shelving units, or complicated container systems, your life would iron itself out. It won't. You may end up with many trendy tools, but you'll still be exhausted, bankrupt, and no less submerged than before. You probably don't need to be more organized. You might just need to own less stuff. You might just need to declutter.

Despite what the design shows would have you believe, organizing and decluttering are not the same things. Organizing is problem-solving. Decluttering is getting rid of the problem. Organizing is shifting the mess to a different space or wrapping it in a pretty package. But in the end, you still own the mess. It's just wearing a high-priced bow to look better.

Here are five simple rules to help you consider what, if anything, to get rid of (donate, regift, recycle, or throw away) when you feel burdened by too much stuff:

The One–Year Rule

If you haven't used an item in a year and it holds no emotional or relational value because of who gave it to you or under what circumstances it was given, get rid of it. The past is a great indicator of the future. If you haven't used it in more than a year, chances are high that you won't ever use it again.

The 20/20 Rule

If you are not using an item (or don't plan to use it in the next six to twelve months) and are confident it will cost less than twenty dollars or twenty minutes to replace, get rid of it. You can part with it with less regret, knowing that should you ever need or want it in the future, you can replace it easily. (Spoiler alert: You probably won't even think of it again.)

The One-In-Two-Out Rule

Any time you purchase a new-to-you item, commit to removing two items of similar size, type, or purpose from your home. For instance, if you buy a new pair of jeans, get rid of two pairs you no longer wear.

The Boundaries Rule

Your space (room, storage organizer, cupboard, or drawer) is a finite boundary and a helpful friend when you are overwhelmed. If an item doesn't fit its container, it needs to go. This is especially true when you own a large collection of similar items. For instance, if your hair clips continue to spill out of their assigned bin, it's time to declutter. Dump them out onto a counter. Pick your favorite clip and place it back into the bin. Then, pick your next favorite. Continue choosing hair clips in order from most to least favorite. Once the bin is full, permanently discard any clips that remain on the counter. This method ensures you not only keep fewer things but you keep the things that matter most.

The Smallest-Stones-First Rule

When decluttering an entire room, start with the least sentimental items first. It's easier to make a fast, efficient decision about something when you don't have a memory attached to it. By weeding out inconsequential goods first, you'll make an instant dent in the clutter, feel the benefits of a more ordered space, and be more mentally prepared to tackle the nostalgic items that will take more time and attention to weed through.

4

Live in Your Season

When you make a choice, you accept the limitations of that choice. To accept limitation requires maturity.
ELISABETH ELLIOT

I sat across from a young mom in a hipster coffee shop, the kind that serves deconstructed breakfast sandwiches in a bowl for around the price of the down payment of a tiny house. We went to the same church, and although we had known of each other for quite some time, this was our first real conversation.

If you were to chart our lives on a Venn diagram, there would be a surprisingly large amount of overlap. Like me, she was a writer. She had a growing social media presence, had just signed her first book deal, and had aspirations of homeschooling her toddler someday. We were both southern transplants to a northern area, and even after living here for several years, we were still not quite fluent in the special peculiarities of the language of the Midwest. We were the same in many ways, with one minor exception. She was about twelve years my junior.

Aside from the noticeable physical differences that an age gap of that magnitude reveals—namely, her body parts didn't yet droop or give her sad feelings—it was clear she was in a completely different stage of mothering. She had one toddler still in diapers, hadn't enjoyed a complete night's sleep in nearly two years, and looked as if she could be the ringleader of the over-caffeinated stroller mafia who sprinted through the park every Thursday morning. Like them, she wore the face of a woman desperate for encouragement and adult interaction.

I, on the other hand, had a house full of tweens and teens, all of whom could successfully wipe their own bottoms and who no longer required me to cut up their meat at dinner. I could take a bath at my leisure without the threat of a little hand under the door wiggling for my attention and could run a quick errand without lugging along a small arsenal of "just in case" clothes, snacks, and toys. Obviously, mothering my older kids required commitment and self-sacrifice. But because they were much older, they were all remarkably self-sufficient.

As I sat across from this young mom, I was more than aware of our different mothering seasons. My kids still needed me. They just needed me in less relentless ways. Even with a fully committed husband by her side to help carry the load, this woman was in the mom-heavy years of mothering. To the casual observer, our lives may have looked quite similar, but in reality we were poles apart.

With a pencil poised in one hand, ready to jot down whatever scheduling hacks I lobbed her way, she asked the million-dollar question every overwhelmed young mother has wondered at one time or another, myself included, "How did you do it all when you had little ones?"

"I didn't," was my flat reply.

Clearly, it was not the answer she was hoping for. She had taken time from her busy schedule to learn my winning strategies for maintaining balance, and my advice was aggressively underwhelming.

"*Balance* is a spotted unicorn," I said. "A mythical creature that exists only in fairy tales, especially in the toddler years." I couldn't have been clearer about my position if I had explained it using sock puppets, yet she stared at me in utter confusion. I wasn't trying to be glib or uncaring. I only wanted her to see that her dreams of being a public speaker, best-selling author, or even church ministry leader, while good, may not necessarily have been good for her right then. Just as different seasons of creation force us to live differently—eat foods when they are ripe, participate in activities according to the weather, and shift our energies for times of growth and times of rest—the seasons of mothering require us to live differently too.

Living Lasts a Lifetime

As women, we can often fall into a scarcity mindset. We fixate on what we can't do instead of fully appreciating what God's given us to do right now. This may be especially true for young mothers, like this one, whose days are determined by the needs of those in their care.

As it happens, living lasts a lifetime. If the Proverbs 31 Woman has taught us anything, it's that it doesn't all need to be done in this season. When we speak of her, we often do so in hushed reverent tones, focusing our attention on the fact that she was diligent, industrious, and self-controlled. A matriarch of motherhood, she was the gold standard of women. One glance her way can be a bit demoralizing.

We fixate on what we can't do instead of fully appreciating what God's given us to do right now.

If your inner critic is anything like mine, I'd venture to guess that every time you open to that particular place in Proverbs, you begin to hiss a few choice words under your breath about how you don't and won't ever measure up. You allow this icon of the faith to cast a shadow over your motherhood, forgetting two essential parts of her story.

First, the woman mentioned in Proverbs 31 wasn't a real woman. She was more of a composite example of many godly women made up by King Lemuel's mother. Like a character in a childhood nursery rhyme, the lady of Proverbs was a caricature captured in an acrostic poem to help a young boy learn what kind of woman to look for when choosing a wife someday. Hers was the "Little Red Hen" fable of the day—a memorable recitation with a thinly veiled moral lesson. Her life was meant to be an inspiration, not a blueprint.

Second, the woman of Proverbs 31 wasn't young. She was a seasoned mother with many miles of life behind her. It's tempting to read how she selected wool and flax, bought a field and planted a vineyard, cared for the poor, sewed linen garments to sell, and then assume she did all of that while pregnant and toting a toddler on her hip. Likely, she didn't. Most scholars agree that Proverbs 31:10–31 is a look back. It's an accounting of decades of growth, change, and maturation. It's not a snapshot of a moment but an album of many years. Her story should compel us toward contentment through every season of motherhood—to accept the limitations of the moment.

Boundaries Aren't Bad

Sadly, at times, I struggled against the boundaries young children placed in my life. In the early years of mothering, I longed for more—the promotion at work, an invitation to lead the women's Bible study, the book deal. Anytime an opportunity came along, I assumed I had to crowbar it into my already busy life or I'd forfeit it forever. I felt strangled by the responsibilities of the right here, right now.

But the truth is, boundary lines are not constricting. According to

Scripture, they are drawn to give us the portion we need presently. They point us to our inheritance—God. Psalm 16:5–11 reads,

> Lord, you alone are my portion and my cup;
> you make my lot secure.
> The boundary lines have fallen for me in pleasant places;
> surely I have a delightful inheritance.
> I will praise the Lord, who counsels me;
> even at night my heart instructs me.
> I keep my eyes always on the Lord.
> With him at my right hand, I will not be shaken. (NIV)

The words *portion, lot, lines,* and *inheritance* are taken right from the Torah, the first five books of the Old Testament, and elicit images of the birthright God gave to the people of Israel when they entered into the promised land. When Moses divided the countryside into plots, he gave each tribe their portion—their inheritance. Just like the property lines that separated the land of one Hebrew clan from that of the next, the time, energy, and financial constraints of your particular season are not hemming you in; they are helping to create healthy boundaries between you and the rest of the world. Boundaries guard valuable things. They protect you. They keep all the extra worries and concerns of other seasons out. Setting a boundary is an admission that you are a finite being. Although it is a purposeful limitation, it's not limiting. A boundary is a legacy—the portion—that God has set aside, especially for you.

Regrettably, in the active years of mothering littles, I was often guilty of missing the inheritance of the moment because it was disguised as regular life—the first bike ride without training wheels, the popsicles on the front porch after a disappointing Little League game, the dandelion bouquet presented by chubby preschool fingers. I now realize that these and so many other seemingly mundane experiences are the wonders of the world—the greatest hits of my life.

A boundary is a legacy—the portion—that God has set aside, especially for you.

It is in the unseen work of motherhood that our faith is formed. The physical, emotional, and even spiritual sacrifices required to raise children may not leave much room for other commitments, but if that is the work that God has given you to do, it is holy work. It is your chance to display both obedience to and worship of your King. It is work that will reap eternal rewards.

The inconvenience and sacrifices of *right now* can be a daily reminder of Christ's most inconvenient sacrifice. In laying down His life for us, Jesus gave us an eternal inheritance. Constrained by the flesh of humanity, His self-imposed boundary became our hope. As a mother, the boundaries of raising children might feel limiting, but they are actually an opportunity to follow Christ's example—to live within the will of the Father and the portion He has for you.

Planting vs. Harvesting

Young mom, you may have to lay down your dream or passion projects for a time but rest assured, they are not going anywhere. Unless the Lord wills, the life you have now will not be the life you will have forever. There will be plenty of new and different "portions" for you someday. In the meantime, you can prepare for a good harvest by establishing the kind of home culture that can support and nurture the fruit you hope to grow.

Be wary of self-inflicted overwhelm. In the early years when just getting your children out the door takes herculean effort, avoid the cultural pressure to sign them up for every club, activity, or team. Is there anything inherently wrong with ballet, tumbling, chess team, robotics, baseball, piano, theatre, horseback riding, or fill-in-the-blank-hobby? Not necessarily. But if your child's participation in any or all of these puts you into a survival defensive crouch each and every day, it's probably time to pare back the activities schedule. Say no. Stay home. Additionally, if you are crowbarring more and more preoccupations into their schedule in an effort to avoid the necessary but commonplace work of discipleship and training, I'd urge you to rethink your priorities and home culture.

Culture is *cultura* in Latin and means the "act of preparing the earth for crops."[1] Any farmer will be quick to mention that throwing seeds at a patch of earth won't ensure a healthy harvest come fall. Those seeds have to be planted with intentionality, watered, nurtured, and protected from predators. It takes time for things to grow. It takes patience. It takes dedication. It takes laying aside other good work to do the very best work.

Every time you answer the cries of a teething baby at too-early o'clock in the morning, show a kindergartener how to properly make his bed for the twelfth day in a row, or say no to the distracting demands of unnecessary after-school activities, you are planting seeds and digging in deep roots that will produce a harvest you'll be able to draw from for the rest of your days. The hidden life of mothering little ones is producing the kind of maturity and clarity that will be needed in the next season for both you and them.

At times, you may see tiny buds of character sprouting—small reminders of what is growing—but only after you've taken the time to train, disciple, and model those qualities yourself. Be careful not to rush the process.

Mothering is a long game that requires daily, repetitive faithfulness. You wash the same dishes every day. You answer the same questions every day. You pick up the same toys every day. It's never glamorous and rarely easy. But it's worth it. Scripture puts it this way, "And let us not grow weary of doing good, for in due season we will reap, if we do not give up" (Gal. 6:9). You can't expect a harvest during planting season. The ground might seem barren and fallow right now with little to nothing to show for your efforts of training and discipling, but the harvest will come. Just keep planting.

When Your Season No Longer Serves You

Perhaps you are no longer wrangling little kids. Maybe, like me, you have a house full of almost-adults and are still grasping for a mothering space you've outgrown. You ache for a return of simple solutions—when a band-aid could cover up every wound and a nap or a snack was the snake-oil cure-all for most complaints. Fearing the future, you continue to cling to the systems and stuff of the past even when they no longer serve you. You straddle both seasons, trying to carry all the routines, expectations, and even control from those early years into this new time and place. As a result, *overwhelm* lurks in the shadows of your days. Please know you are not alone, friend. Endings are hard. They feel like *loss*. But rest assured, God will always meet you in the dust. He will catch your tears and cover your disappointments with His comfort.

I'm currently smack dab in the middle of this very growth-grief. Once upon a time, I felt comfortable in my mothering skin. I was the Fun Mom, the Fearless Mom, the Worry-free Mom. I hosted the backyard tea parties, the neighborhood sledding socials, and the tree-climbing tournaments. I took my crew to the park, the library, and the splash pad, sometimes all on the same day. I happily let them learn to whittle, make the paper-mache piñatas, and build the giant bike ramps. I was determined to squeeze every drop of courage and togetherness out of our days.

Now I have teenagers and young adults who couldn't care less about carving pumpkins, who have jobs and aren't always around for impromptu hikes in the woods or backyard picnics, and who'd rather have one more hour of sleep than get up early to grab donuts together. They drive, make life-altering decisions, and are slowly unmooring themselves from me and our home. Two of my children have moved out. One is attending college on the other side of the continent, and another has recently joined the armed forces. The national and global news can leave me paralyzed with panic for them both. As their lives expand, mine recedes. As they launch with hopeful anticipation, I tremble in fear over the many *what-ifs*. Doomsday thoughts begin to burrow, leaving no rock unturned. So much for courage and togetherness.

Have I portrayed my life in Christ in a compelling way? Will they hold fast to their faith? Will they face our decaying culture with boldness and determination? Will they love God and love others well? And also, will they remember to call home every now and again? I don't just want to know that they will be okay. I want their good futures guaranteed, notarized, and sent with email confirmation.

Every day, I'm faced with a choice. I can clench all my plans for them tight in my fists, forcing my teens to keep-up-or-else, or I can find ways to be the mom they need in this new season. I can hold them hostage in my home or set them free to do God's big and sometimes dangerous work for such a time as this. In other words, I can spend my life mourning the death of what *was*, or I can fully embrace the life of what *is*. I can become immobilized in my anxiety, or I can release them to God, who loves them far more than I ever can or ever will.

If I'm completely honest, mothering teens and young adults has been a two-step-forward, one-step-back kind of dance. The big emotions and worldview-forming conversations that come with adolescence can leave me feeling raw, like I've been skinned alive by a veggie peeler. When my kids were young, I was a fountain pouring out to them. Now that they

Overwhelmed Mom

are older, I have become a well for them to draw from. This new season is less physically taxing but just as draining in other ways. (*Why do teens want to have deep theological conversations after midnight? Don't they know I'm past forty?*) The spiritual and mental demands have forced me to write a new mothering manifesto—one that requires me to let go of what I've been holding on to and also what has been holding onto me.

> I can relinquish control.
> I can appreciate who they are now but also who they are becoming.
> I can allow them to grow.
> I can respect their desire not to have their picture taken.
> I can relinquish control.
> I can let them fail.
> I can stand with them when they face the consequences of their actions.
> I can relinquish control.
> I can listen more and speak less.
> I can cheer them on in their passions even when their interests are nothing like my own.
> I can ask for their opinions and value their answers even when I disagree.
> I can relinquish control.
> I can let them go, believing they'll always come home again.
> I can stop force-feeding my faith into them and trust that God is big enough to hold their questions and curiosities.
> I can free them to His loving care.
> I can relinquish control.
> I can allow good things to end to see great things begin.
> I can relinquish control.

My time left with my teens should get a speeding ticket. It's going by so quickly. Whenever I'm tempted to hold them too closely or squeeze them too tightly, I am reminded of the words of children's teacher and Christian writer Ashlei Woods, who wrote, "There comes a time—many times, actually—in the lives of our children when we have to put the basket in the water. We have to let go and trust the plan of the Father. The world is a scary place—a place where we fear our children could drown. But we must remember that we have to let go so that God can draw them from the waters for His great purpose. He has called us to be their parents, but they were His first."[2]

I don't know what waters I'll be required to place my children into in the coming days, months, and years of their lives, but I know God will go with them and draw them out in His good time. I don't need to allow any of the unknowns to create anxiety or overwhelm in my life. First, though, I must let go of their baskets. I must turn my *what-if* worries into *even-if* worship. I can relinquish control.

Each season of motherhood will demand that I choose good, better, and best. Each season will require me to ask, "What do I need to release? Which version of my motherhood do I need to say goodbye to? What expectations have I kept that I must finally let go?" The same can be said for you, Overwhelmed Mom.

Contrary to what the culture has been telling us for the past three decades, we can't do everything at the same time or even at all. Neither can our kids. Some things may very well be good but not necessarily good for right now or for always. Regardless of what season of mothering you and I are in, we'll both find more contentment and less chaos if we're willing to be present right here, right now. Let's not waste another moment fixating on the future or pining for the past. Let's learn to live in our season.

Things to Ponder

1. What season of mothering are you in right now?

2. What are the limitations of this particular season? What are the boundary lines God has placed in your life currently? On an average day, how do you feel about the portion He has given you?

3. What are you pining for from the past? What are you fixating on for the future?

4. Read Ecclesiastes 9:10 and Colossians 3:17 and 23, and consider how your current work, both inside and outside the home, can be worship to God.

5. Is there a commitment in your child's life that is creating or exacerbating your current overwhelm? Ask God to give you wisdom regarding your child's continuation of that commitment.

6. What kind of fruit are you beginning to see in the lives of your kids? Name a time God gave you a glimpse of the work He is doing through you in their maturation and sanctification.

Wisdom from God's Word

Proverbs 31
Ecclesiastes 3:1–8
Galatians 6:9

The Motherload: Shopping & Errands

When you're overwhelmed, even a commonplace errand like dropping packages off at the post office can feel like an oppressive taskmaster. One minute, you're standing in a never-ending line, hoping the giant box you're balancing precariously on your hip won't kill you. And the next minute, you're so frustrated with the slow-moving pace of the room that you begin praying it will.

I, for one, would rather eat a bag of hair than run errands of any kind. And don't even get me started on my feelings about the mall. That place gives me hostile thoughts even on a good day. But even if you typically consider shopping and making deliveries a relaxing event, during a busy season, these small tasks can sometimes leave you seeing double. Here are a few simple tips to help you be the most efficient while running errands.

Replenish; Don't Unpack

In the same way that you probably set aside a specific bag for diapers when you had a baby, designate separate bags for all your other habitual activities, including going to the library, the beach, music lessons, church, homeschool co-op, and even short work trips. Each regular activity should be assigned its own bag. Fill each one with the items needed for its corresponding function and nothing else. Unless they are used daily, store these bags out of the way until needed. Whenever you have to take something out of the bag, return it after its use or replace it immediately. Don't unpack the entire bag. Just replenish and return its contents.

Bag Groceries with Un–bagging in Mind

Assume you will not be able to unpack all your groceries when you get home from the store. Expect to be interrupted by a baby who needs to be nursed or a tween who needs help finding her baseball cleats before practice. With this in mind, while at the grocery store checkout, pack your groceries according to where you will permanently store them. Pack freezer items in the same bag(s), fridge items in a different bag(s), and pantry or non-perishable items in still different bag(s). When you get home, unpack the freezer and fridge bags first, knowing you can leave the pantry bags for later if you need to. That way, no matter how long it takes to put everything in its proper place, none of your groceries will spoil. If you, like me, have more than one freezer or pantry area, pack so that as you carry groceries into your house, you can immediately deposit them in front of or near their storage space in preparation for unpacking them.

Stock Up when Prices Are Down

Create a master list of the everyday prices of all the grocery items you typically buy. Organize it in sections according to store departments (produce, meat, dairy, etc.). Be sure to include the price per pound for things like meat, cheese, and produce. Keep this list in the car or on your phone so it's easily accessible when you're running errands. Whenever you see something that looks to be on sale and that has a long shelf-life or can be easily frozen for later, compare the sale price to your master list for assurance that it is, in fact, a good deal, and then buy a large quantity. A well-stocked pantry and freezer will not only save you money, it will also save you time as it saves trips to the grocery store. Instead, you'll be able to shop from your own shelves.

Plan an Efficient Route

As much as possible, assign your errands, including doctor or salon appointments, to one particular day, preferably a weekday when stores are less crowded. Before heading out, make a mental map of your route to prevent doubling back through town unnecessarily. If feasible, keep a cooler in your trunk so that you can store perishable groceries in your car if you need to make additional stops before heading home.

Don't Use a Cart

If you only need to buy a few items at one store, don't use a cart or basket. Carry your items to the cashier counter by hand. The cumbersome weight and awkward volume of your purchases will discourage you from spending too much time browsing in the store and splurging on items not on your list. If it can't be carried, it can't be bought.

5

Choose Your Hard

Do few things, but do them well. Simple joys are holy.
COMMONLY ATTRIBUTED TO ST. FRANCIS OF ASSISI

I was hunched over a cardboard box in a neighborhood gymnasium, unpacking gently used household items recently donated for the spring fundraising yard sale of my son's baseball team, when one of the other volunteers casually asked for my wheat bread recipe.

"Sure thing," I said. "I just made a loaf before I left the house tonight. I'm pretty sure I forgot to put the recipe away. When I get home, I'll take a picture of it and text it to you." This short exchange unleashed an avalanche of probing questions—an interrogation, really.

"You made a loaf of bread? Tonight? In the middle of the week?" the woman to my right asked. "You must be a slave to the kitchen!" Like most of the other mothers gathered to set up for the sale, she was a casual acquaintance I knew from our shared spot in the bleachers during game season.

"It must be nice to have the time to make homemade bread on a weekday. Some of us have to work for a living," another woman chimed in. "Around my house, I cook dinner. That's it. I have teenagers, and they are old enough to fend for themselves for breakfast and lunch."

"Let me get this straight: You made bread just before coming here to do all of this?" a woman on the other side of the gym questioned, sweeping her arms wide over our many organized tables while raising her eyebrows in shock. Or was it judgment? The lines between the two are so often blurred.

"I made two, actually," I mumbled. "We ate one with soup for dinner, and I set the other aside for French toast in the morning."

My simple reply made the sorting and pricing come to a halt. Hands stilled. Dusty donations were forgotten. A hush swept over the room as if I had just confessed to running an illegal sports-betting ring from the team snack bar.

"She cooks three full meals a day. Every single day. From scratch," the recipe-seeker said, trying to defuse my discomfort by speaking up on my behalf. Bless her. She had no idea I'd had this same discussion many times before. Maybe not with these particular women or about this particular confession. Nonetheless, the exchange was the same. Serving three homemade meals a day for my family seemed always to be an unpardonable sin in most women's circles.

In the past when others have heard about my focus on feeding my family, I've received caustic comments.

"Don't you think you're spoiling them?"

"I prefer the yoyo method. You're On Your Own, kiddos."

"Wow! That sounds complicated. Doesn't your husband ever help in the kitchen? Is he one of those patriarchal types?"

Sometimes commenters feign support, draping their encouragement over covert criticism.

"Good for you! If I had that much time on my hands, I'd make more meals from scratch."

"You know, you could serve leftovers for lunch and not have to be in the kitchen so much. Plus, you wouldn't have to scrub pots and pans twice. Hope that helps!"

As has often been the case, no one in the gym seemed to hear me when I said I didn't do *all* the cooking—that my kids often took turns making one of the meals each day, or that because of the size of my family, I rarely had leftovers sitting around, or that I loved cooking and saw it as an outlet for my own creativity, or even that I considered the act of serving food to those I loved less about fueling their bodies and more about nourishing their lives and helping them thrive. No one listened to my reasons because they were too busy forming their own conclusions. At best, these women saw me as an overachiever; at worst, they assumed I was being manipulated in my own home.

Neither could be further from the truth. I'm aggressively average in so many areas of my life, but feeding people is where I shine. I do food well. Not to say that providing three nutritious meals a day is always easy or even convenient. Nothing worth pursuing will ever come without some amount of effort. Some days, I'd rather just pull up to a window and order something greasy to go. But investing my time and energy in the kitchen is a choice I have made. It is a *yes* that, while challenging at times, has been said on purpose. It's a priority to me.

Misaligned Priorities

I can care about many things, but I cannot do many things with care. The good news is, I get to decide. I get to choose my *hard*—the tasks that will require more of my attention, commitment, and sweat. I get to intentionally promote the things I value most and ignore anything that detracts from them. The same can be said for all the baseball-team moms.

The numerous iterations of "I don't have time for that" we hear often, or even make ourselves, are gross exaggerations and can even be unintentional lies. A person will make time for what is important to them. That includes me. That includes you, too. Always. That's just the nature of humanity. The opposite of people-pleasing isn't not caring; it is caring about the right things. It's holding care with confidence. Intentional selection is to be commended. Instead of blaming lack of time as the reason we are not committing to something, we should admit that we are choosing to spend our minutes differently and say, "That's not a priority for me right now." Most will welcome and applaud that honesty and sincere confession.

I can care about many things, but I cannot do many things with care.

Cooking was clearly not high on anyone else's to-do list in the gym that evening. Fair enough. I carried no hard feelings when I left because I knew that many of those women spent their time doing worthwhile work that I was ill-equipped or uninterested in doing, like growing prize-winning azaleas, running multiple 5Ks each year, or performing cleft-palate surgery in third-world countries. I didn't begrudge or belittle any of these wins in their lives because I knew someone else's success in an area was not a threat to me and my giftings.

The point is, for the most part, every yard-sale volunteer had the privilege of deciding what mattered to her—and so do you. You don't play a supporting role in your own life, friend. You're not a sidekick or a wingman. Peace in your home won't usually come just because you're hoping for it. More often than not, it will come when you've planned for it—when you've not just given an indifferent *yes* but have leaned hard into a task—even a difficult one—with no regrets, when you've decided what is important enough to spend some of your life on.

In many cases, feeling stressed, frazzled, or frayed is a good indicator of misaligned priorities. Overwhelm is often a sign that you've chosen the wrong *hard* or ranked your commitments incorrectly.

You may have many plates to spin, but I'll bet they are not all made of the same material. Probably some of your responsibilities are more important or more delicate overall than others. They are like china plates. Others are significant but do not hold the same value in the grand scheme of your life as those in the former group. These responsibilities are like glass or stoneware plates. Still others are trivial extras that, while fun or meaningful for a moment, don't begin to compare in worth to any of your other obligations. These responsibilities are like plastic or even paper plates. Do you see where I'm going with this analogy?

You must first determine the merit of each plate and then spin it accordingly, knowing that certain ones can be dropped and picked up again when necessary, without completely shattering the whole lot. Obviously, your china plates will require your best attention, your most effort, and your most significant amount of life equity.

Your responsibilities will look vastly different from mine. You may be in a season of life that prohibits any extra commitments. (I'm looking at you, young mom of babies and tots.) On the flip side, you may operate at a much higher capacity than me. Your plate-spinning ability may rival that of a vaudeville act. Your life is as unique as you are. But since I know how helpful it can be to see a nebulous idea fleshed out in a real-life example, I'll give you a quick peek at my current commitments and how I have ranked them to dedicate an appropriate amount of attention to each.

My China Plates
Worshiping and obeying Jesus
Loving my husband
Caring for my children

My Glass or Stoneware Plates
Advocating for my mother, who has dementia
Homeschooling my children
Nurturing my relationships with a handful of close friends
Earning an income through writing and speaking

My Plastic Plates
Serving nutritious meals to family and friends
Leading a local homeschool co-op
Tending my relationships with a broader circle of friends, acquaintances, and other image bearers
Volunteering at the local soup kitchen
Maintaining a clean-ish home

My Paper Plates
Greeting and registering families for children's church
Leading a teen book club
Hosting a women's book club

This is obviously not an exhaustive list. There are other minor or more infrequent demands on my time. But for the most part, anytime I feel overwhelmed, I can analyze my plates to determine which ones I can drop while still honoring my priorities.

Ranking my commitments also helps me see how I've let specific responsibilities command too much authority in my life. If baking homemade bread occupies so much of my attention that I don't have time to nourish my children's hearts with the truth of Scripture, then I have misaligned priorities. If creating elaborately themed birthday parties for my friends steals so much of my time that I can't actually sit with the one being celebrated, I have misaligned priorities. If my home is so spotless that my husband and children live in fear of suffering my wrath should they make a mess, I have misaligned priorities. When I don't prioritize my work, the most important things end up at the bottom of the pile, and I spend all my time and energy on the urgent but less important tasks. You too?

Jesus showed us the way to prioritize our time. He never succumbed to the tyranny of the urgent or fast-walked through life. He chose the more important work. Mark 1:35–39 describes how, after healing the sick and casting out demons the night before, Jesus rose early one morning to spend some time in private prayer. He withdrew to a quiet spot alone. Seeing the pressing needs of the growing crowds, Simon Peter rallied a search party to find Him and bring Him back. "Everyone is looking for you," he declared to the Lord. Instead of performing more medical miracles, Jesus suggested they go to the neighboring towns to preach. "For that is why I came out," He said.

> *When I don't prioritize my work, the most important things end up at the bottom of the pile.*

John 11:1–43 tells how, when He learned that His friend Lazarus was ill, Jesus did not rush off to restore his health. The urgent need was healing, something He was fully able to do. But curing a head cold or a nasty stomach bug would have been like fixing a leaky faucet in a burning building—futile. Instead, Jesus wanted to build the faith of His followers. In allowing Lazarus to die, Christ revealed His power to overcome death.

In both instances, the spiritual needs of the people were far more important than their urgent physical needs. There was an order to the Lord's commitments that showed His priorities. He came to this earth with a mission and set His gaze on that work. Even with the mounting distractions surrounding him, Jesus had laser focus. He never let the urgent eclipse the most important.

Make It Your Mission

But how do you determine your priorities? How can you honor your mission and give your best attention to what matters most? The fact is, there should be very little disconnect between your values and your ventures. The former is what you believe; the latter is what you do. When those two don't align, neither one is worth anything. Further, *overwhelm* will almost always follow.

Determining your core values before you have to give a *yes* or *no* to something will not necessarily make the choice clear, but it will surely make the decision less fuzzy.

Just as a mission statement can help to clarify the goals and narrow the focus of a business, a personal vision statement can help you illuminate your priorities and refine how you spend your time. It can create boundaries for decision-making. It won't necessarily forecast what your life or home will be like in twenty years. You can't control the future, so why waste time planning for circumstances that are out of your hands? Instead, a vision statement creates a picture of what you want your life and your home to be like right now.

When crafting a personal vision statement, think about who you are. If you're reading this book, you're probably a mother, but what else? *Mom* is not your only name. Are you a wife, a friend, a Christian, a teacher, an artist? Make a short inventory of your names or titles.

Here is a peek at my current names.

I am a
Child of God
Wife
Mother
Teacher
Writer
Speaker

Then, consider your people and your passions. Who is in your sphere of influence, and what skills can you employ to serve them best? Brainstorm a list of all the people who command a portion of your attention. Include family members, neighbors, friends, work connections, ministry partners, and church community. Don't be afraid to add the names of people who you don't currently impact but who you naturally feel a tug toward.

My personal list looks like this:

I am privileged to serve
Dain (my husband)
Maddie, Reese, Finnlae, Jack, and Jude (my children)
My extended family
A small circle of close friends
My neighbors
Local church members
Local and national homeschool moms

Next, jot down your skills, past experiences, abilities, and God-given passions. Those last two can often be tricky to identify, especially when you feel like your life is a tinder box and one more point of friction will ignite the whole thing, leaving you with nothing but ash. The idea of chasing one's passions can feel privileged and impractical. But it's not. It's actually a form of worship. It's a way of saying, "Creator God, You have fashioned me uniquely so I may bring You glory in specific ways." Using your giftings and passions for His purposes is one way to fight against the darkness and decay of this world, bringing order not just in your life but in the lives of others.

It's helpful to ask, "What can I talk about for an hour with little to no preparation? What am I good at? What do people often ask me for advice about or look to me to manage?" Make a list of five to ten activities that come naturally to you. These strengths are your social assets—the contributions or legacies you're known best for. Examples of social assets might include the following:

Baking
Building or repairing
Caring for the physical needs of others
Creating natural home health products
Decorating or designing beautiful spaces
Grooming pets
Hair styling
Homesteading
Investing
Mobilizing people
Organizing spreadsheets
Painting
Sewing
Solving math equations
Studying the Bible

My personal list includes the following:

I am skilled in
Baking bread
Curating book lists for kids
Encouraging others in their giftings
Mentoring
Performing administrative tasks
Speaking to large crowds
Teaching
Writing

Now it's time to put the three lists together to create a one-sentence statement that tells who you are, who you serve, and how you serve them. You'll not be able to include every item on each of your lists. Instead, use this simple formula to combine and summarize them into a succinct sentence that can be easily set to memory: *I am a [your most important names] who serves [people/groups] by [skills/passions]*.

Feel free to go off-script and create your own formula. Just be sure to articulate the three primary parts: who you are, who you serve, and how you best serve them. A vague vision statement benefits no one, least of all you. So be specific. This is *your* legacy. That's not to say that a vision statement never changes. Most likely, some of the goals of a single woman will change once she gets married. A mother of littles will need to tweak her plans a bit after her kids are grown and launched. That's to be expected. You're allowed to change your mind, to grow, and to have new and different priorities. Remember, a vision statement is about the present. It's about what you want your impact to be right now.

My current personal vision statement reads like this:

Jamie Erickson is a Christian wife and mother passionate about mentoring other moms toward intentional motherhood by providing tools and resources to help them grow their faith, organize their time, teach and train their kids, and create a hospitable home.

My statement speaks specifically about who I am, who I minister to, and how I minister, but it is general enough to apply to many situations. Now when I'm asked to help organize a pledge drive for the local animal shelter, I can give a kind but unapologetic *no* because I can see how that particular commitment, albeit honorable, does not align with my vision. On the flip side, when a neighbor asks if I can watch her toddler three days a week until she can find more permanent childcare, I'll be able to quickly recognize how that task might be well worth my time investment.

A vision statement will force you to *determine* before you have to *decide*. Essentially, it will help you curate your time in the same way that a museum curator selects art for an exhibit. There are thousands of great creative works worth displaying. It's a curator's job, however, to select the pieces that best represent the theme, artist, medium, or time period she wants to showcase, all while considering the limitations of her space and budget. She has to intentionally bypass the *good* to leave room for the *best*.

Determine Your Yes

Even after giving voice to your priorities in a well-crafted vision statement, you may still struggle to sift through opportunities. Some decisions may require an agonizing amount of deliberation. At first, my neighbor's request that I fill in as a temporary babysitter may seem like a no-brainer *yes* for me. It certainly appears to align with my priorities. Not only would I be able to provide a safe space for a little one, which is certainly one way to model hospitality, but I'd also have a daily influence on both mother and child, which would, no doubt, deepen our relationships.

And yet, when asked, I almost always waffle between wanting to say no and feeling guilty for not saying yes. *Am I being selfish in thinking such thoughts? Wouldn't serving my neighbor in this way be a good use of my time? Wouldn't I be stewarding my days well as Ephesians 5:16 and 1 Peter 4:10 charge?* I wonder. Does this sound at all familiar? If so, rest assured: Overthinking may be a cultural contagion, but it's also a curable one. You'll find the remedy tucked safely in the pages of Paul's letter to the church of Philippi. In Philippians 1:9–10, he writes, "And this is my prayer: that your love may abound more and more in knowledge and depth of insight, so that you may be able to discern what is best and may be pure and blameless for the day of Christ" (NIV).

My apologies for sounding like a 1980s televangelist, but if it's discernment you seek, then in the power of the Spirit, ask for it. Don't waste one more minute drowning in what-about-isms. Bring your questions and concerns to God in prayer. Come to Him in bold humility, asking for wisdom, and as James 1:5–6 promises, He will give it generously and without reproach. He is for you. He wants the best for you. Call upon God to be true to His Word, and He will be.

One of the surest paths to feeling overwhelmed is a lack of information. So, as you hold your hands open to God, asking Him to provide a peace that passes all understanding regarding the decision you're facing, begin to ask yourself some clarifying questions.

For example, when determining how best to answer my neighbor, I should consider the following:

Do I have the time to watch a toddler three days a week? The energy?
How long will the commitment last? One month? Six? A year?
Do I have a toddler-friendly home with ample toys and equipment suitable for her needs?
Will my own children begrudge the intrusion?
What about when I must pick up and drop off my teen from his summer job? Will I need to buy or borrow a car seat?

Your particular situation must be examined through your specific set of circumstances.

Here is a list of universally applicable questions to help simplify your decision-making and guide you to a thoughtful response. Maybe one or two of these questions will bring you clarity as you face a decision about using your time and gifts.

Does Scripture have anything specific to say about this situation?
What is the kingdom purpose of this?
Will this bear fruit for Christ?
What are my true motivations behind my yes or no?
Does this opportunity fit my Christian worldview?
Does it seem logical?
Will a yes put me in financial debt?
Will a yes cause my current relationships or commitments to suffer?
Will a yes put too much stress on other areas of my life?
Where does this opportunity fit with my current vision statement or priorities?

What does my spouse think about the situation?

What does my pastor (doctor, coworkers, or other professionals in my field) think?

What is the worst that could happen?

What do I stand to gain/lose in saying yes or no?

Do I need to put any contingencies in place or create an exit plan?

Can I choose through a process of elimination and/or a pros and cons list?

Is this a proactive decision or a reactive one?

How does this align with my short- and/or long-term goals?

Do I have the skills, tools, or education for this?

Does this align with my spiritual gifts or natural abilities?

Do I have the personality for this opportunity?

Do I have the time, finances, and resources?

Can I give a yes without apologies?

How has a similar yes turned out in the past for me?

What doors have opened already? What doors have closed?

The Hard Yes

The prevailing sentiment in most motherhood circles today seems to be, If it's not a *heck yes*, then it's a *hard no!*[1] In other words, if you don't absolutely love and immediately want to commit to an opportunity, run in the other direction. Run fast. While there is some validity to the idea that a small hesitation on the front end of an answer will only grow larger with time, a knee-jerk response to a hard yes leaves out three fundamental truths of the Christian life.

To begin with, the love of Christ is shown in service—in taking the lower place, deferring to others, and even laying down one's life for another. First John 3:16–18 reads, "By this we know love, that he laid down his life for us, and we ought to lay down our lives for the brothers. But if anyone has the world's goods and sees his brother in need, yet closes his heart against him, how does God's love abide in him? Little children, let us not love in word or talk but in deed and in truth."

In a culture that shouts "You do you!," believers in Christ are called to take up a cross and follow Him. Jesus left the riches of heaven to live in obscurity for most of His earthly life. His yes took Him all the way to the grave. At times, He'll ask us to share and give and pour out our lives too. Whenever we serve in sacrificial ways—when our yes feels costly—we mirror Christ's lavish love to the world.

Next, God sometimes calls us to do hard things because growth rarely happens without growing pains. Hardships produce maturity and clarity. It is often in the refining fire of a difficult task, an unglamorous task, an inconvenient task that our faith in Christ is perfected. First Peter 1:6–7 puts it this way, "In this you rejoice, though now for a little while, if necessary, you have been grieved by various trials, so that the tested genuineness of your faith—more precious than gold that perishes though it is tested by fire—may be found to result in praise and glory and honor at the revelation of Jesus Christ." May we not miss out on the sanctifying work of the Spirit by always opting out of life's ordinary challenges. May we be bold enough to welcome the kind of spiritual growth that can only ever happen when we give a hard yes.

Finally, many tasks are unavoidable and required. We won't always be able to ignore a hard yes under the umbrella of grace. Paying the bills, scrubbing the toilet, refilling prescriptions—these are not jobs anyone clamors to volunteer for—at least not at my house. Why? Because they're uninspiring. To all of us. Yet someone still has to do them.

Our aversion to these and other tedious tasks is proof that, on the whole, everyone wants to build, but very few people want to maintain.

We prefer immediacy—part-time work for full-time pay. We don't want *hard*. We want *easy*. But we must remember that work is not a punishment or a four-letter word. It is a kind gift given

May we not miss out on the sanctifying work of the Spirit by always opting out of life's ordinary challenges.

by God as far back as Eden. In Genesis 2:15, Adam was tasked to work the land. Working was a delight in that first garden home because it was how the creation could worshipfully serve the Creator and enjoy the fruits of their efforts. It wasn't until the fall that work became toilsome.

Sin always has a way of complicating the most pleasurable things, doesn't it? For the believer, work can still be hard. But we can undertake all our tasks with gladness, knowing that any labor done for the Lord is never in vain (Col. 3:23–24). No matter how broken or burdensome our work feels on this side of heaven, it can be restored and redeemed for eternity because of Christ. So lift your work to God. It's worship.

After considering these three aspects of Christlikeness, you may feel convicted to give a hard yes to a venture even when logic and preference make you wish you could give a no. That does not mean you just wedge another time-consuming or physically draining task into your already jam-packed day. Instead, it may require you to strip your schedule down to the studs, scaling back some commitments and permanently dismantling others, at least for a time. That's not side-stepping your responsibility or shirking your duties. The basic laws of physics demand you must take something out of a crowded space before adding something else. If God is calling you to a hard yes in one area of life, He may also be releasing you to give a no to a previously agreed-upon responsibility. Praying about a hard "yes" is an act of surrender.

In the case of my neighbor's appeal, I'll admit I have three very good reasons why I could easily give a guilt-free no to her request: I rarely enjoy babysitting other people's children; I'm currently buried under a book deadline; and I've recently been asked to join the women's ministry leadership team at my church, which definitely feels more life-giving than childcare in my stage of life. But, if after bringing the situation to the Lord, asking for wisdom concerning the part I am to play in this neighbor's need, I can't shake the feeling that this may be a divine appointment both in her life and in mine, I'd be remiss if I did not then ask God to part the waters in my schedule and to show me what I can temporarily set aside. The good news is: He can. He's in the business of making a way when there doesn't seem to be one.

God's in the business of making a way when there doesn't seem to be one.

Overwhelm is often a symptom of overextension—spending your life on trivial tasks that mean nothing to you or squandering your moments on meaningless activities instead of investing time in the crucial ones. You cannot do it all, but you can do what matters. Determine your priorities through prayerful consideration, choose which *hard* is yours to handle, and then be willing to value those commitments by giving them an all-in yes.

Things to Ponder

1. What *hard* commitments currently require your attention, commitment, or sweat? Which, if any, do you feel could be reassessed?

2. Make a list of your current spinning plates. Determine their merit by grouping them into the categories of china, glass, plastic, and paper. Can you relinquish any of the paper

plates so you can keep the more valued plates spinning well?

3. What urgent demands continue to take your attention away from important ones? Consider how you might realign your priorities. Is there a demanding task you can set aside or delegate so you can give more of your time to what matters most to you?

4. Using the simple formula I mentioned, create a personal vision statement. Use it to analyze your current commitments. Do any of your responsibilities fail to align with who you are, who you serve, and how you best serve them?

5. Is there a hard yes you feel the Lord leading you to give? How might you readjust your current schedule to give this new commitment an all-in yes?

Wisdom from God's Word

Ecclesiastes 9:10
Colossians 3:23–24
1 Peter 4:7–11

The Motherload: Menu Planning

"What's for dinner?" If you have tweens or teens in your house, you probably hear this question 3,567 times a day. Even if you answered the query only four minutes ago, your kids will still ask. The fact that three meals a day are a constant can feel like bad news to moms who don't naturally enjoy kitchen duties. But there's good news: Those three meals a day *are* a constant. Even when life shoves many unforeseen circumstances your way, those three mealtimes happen like clockwork. They don't creep up on or surprise you; you already expect them. While other elements of your week range out of your control, for the most part, you can exercise some control over these three seemingly fixed responsibilities each day.

Admittedly, meal planning is one of my favorite home-keeping tasks. Perhaps, like me, just the thought of cooking puts a fire in your belly to whip up something warm and tasty for someone special. Maybe, instead, however, the very idea of stepping foot in the kitchen gives you indigestion. You are not on friendly terms with meal-making, and you'd rather be doing anything else with your time. Fair enough. We're all uniquely wired with preferences and passions. Whether dinner prep feels like fun or forced community service, might I offer you a few tips that have helped me get food on the table a bit easier? I can't guarantee any of these ideas will help you learn to love cooking, but perhaps you'll begin to loathe it a bit less. While I can do most of these digitally with an app, I often get distracted when I'm on my smartphone, which can add to my overwhelm. So I recommend keeping all these suggestions as screen-free as possible.

Make a Meal List, not a Meal Plan

Instead of assigning a meal to a particular day, make a list of seven breakfasts, lunches, and/or dinners you hope to make sometime in the week. Use that plan to create your grocery list to ensure you have all the supplies needed for the entire menu. Then, each morning, choose one breakfast, lunch, and dinner from the list that you know you will have time to make and that sounds good to you in the moment. Remove any items from the freezer that must be thawed by lunch or dinner.

When you make a meal, cross it off the list. The next morning, use the same "What am I craving?" or "What do I have time to make?" system to select three meals from the remaining listed items. Repeat this process each day until all the meals have been crossed off your list. Like a traditional meal plan, a weekly list provides structure but is flexible enough to account for personal daily cravings and pivots in your schedule.

Reverse–Engineer a Meal List

If you struggle to develop a weekly meal list, start from the end and work backward. Instead of writing down what you *want* to eat tomorrow, write down what you *did* eat today. If you keep track for seven consecutive days, you'll have an entire week's worth of meal ideas by the end of the week. Repeat this process for four weeks to create a month-long menu that can be tweaked, rearranged, and improved upon but does not have to be built from the ground up.

Create a Master Menu List

When you have a chunk of time at your disposal, create a personalized-to-you reference work that I like to call the Master Menu List. Write down every main meal you make and divide the list into categories that work for your life, such as the season of the year most appropriate for that dish, the meat or main ingredient used in the preparation (e.g., chicken, beef, pork, fish), the nationality or theme of the dish (e.g., Mexican, Asian, Italian, BBQ), any exclusions that would be important to note (gluten-free, dairy-free, nut-free, etc.), or the occasion that pairs best with that specific recipe (holiday, party, busy night, weekday, potluck). Include the location of that recipe (e.g., Pinterest, cookbook and page number, 3x5 recipe card box) for easy retrievability. Once you have created your main list, add to it as you introduce new recipes to your family.

When you need to make a weekly or monthly menu, you can consult your family calendar to see which evenings will be more chaotic and will require quick-fix dishes. Then use your master list to choose seven main dishes that would work best for that particular week. This helps you be realistic with your time, ensures meal variety, and relieves the mental load required to create a menu.

Store Recipes in One Location

Unless a cookbook is a treasured family collection, resist the temptation to keep it. Cut out or copy the recipes you actually use from each book, store these in clear plastic sleeves in a three-ring binder, and get rid of the original book. Conversely, if you mostly find recipes online, print them out and store them in your binder or create one giant digital folder. In other words, a cookbook collection might look aesthetically pleasing in your kitchen, but in an overwhelming season, a stockpile of books can feel like unnecessary clutter or require too much research time when used. When you have more than one cookbook with a chili recipe and you've forgotten which one contains your family's favorite version, you can spend many precious moments weeding through and trying wrong recipes before rediscovering the right one.

Write a Master Grocery List

Sacrifice an hour this week to walk through your grocery store in the exact order of how you usually shop. List by aisle the items you typically purchase weekly or monthly. Record them in the order you come to them as you walk your typical route through the store.

When you return home, create a simple aisle-by-aisle spreadsheet of this list, leaving a few blank spaces after each aisle for any additional groceries that may not be a standard purchase or are recipe-specific. Print several copies of this list and leave one out each week in a communal space. Then, when anyone in your family notices a grocery need, they can circle or highlight the item on your list to indicate that it needs to be purchased. When you are ready to go shopping, you can ignore the unchecked items on the list and write in extra or unusual groceries you need.

6

Just Start

Pursue a remarkable life by taking a thousand unremarkable steps.
JEFF MANION

You're exactly the mom your kids need you to be." I don't know about you, but I've heard and read this message a lot lately. It's a soothing balm on a day like today when I kept my son at home while a handful of his friends are gathered without him at the local library for their first Lego Robotics club meeting. Ever the extrovert, my youngest desperately wanted to join their budding group, not because he loves STEM, mind you, but because he loves people. Despite his pleas, I did not let him attend. (He's hoping that his assurance that "Everyone else will be there!" punctuated by an entire month's worth of verbal exclamation points will convince me to change my mind on the matter. It won't.)

An extra once-a-week commitment to our schedule would be the fine-line difference between a lively season and an overwhelming one. Guilt lurks in the shadows of my heart even as I write this, knowing that it is because of my desire *not* to overextend our schedules that my son will miss out on the fun. Then I remember, "You're exactly the mom your kids need you to be," and my lingering self-reproach begins to vanish.

While there is comforting truth in that statement, it doesn't tell the whole story. Yes, I am the mom God provided and placed with my five particular children. I am exactly who He knew they'd need. And yet, I'm not fully formed. Growth is still needed. I'll never "arrive" as their mom. I need to keep mastering the skills I've already learned and find ways to learn new ones.

Be a Beginner

For whatever reason, our culture prioritizes training and professional development in so many areas of life but assumes that "winging it" is good enough at home. No wonder we have an entire generation of burned-out moms. Many of us felt ill-equipped and unprepared when we were handed the job. Regrettably, we often still do. Just as you and I may have to take continuing education classes to hone our skills in the workplace, practice new things, and keep current on ever-changing policies, we'd do well to seek professional development for our roles as wives and mothers too.

Two truths can be true at the same time. We can be women who were hand-picked by God to mother our unique children while continuing to grow in the same ways Jesus grew when He walked this earth wearing the flesh of humanity—in wisdom, stature, and favor with both God and man (Luke 2:52).

Right about now, you may be bristling—am I really insinuating that you add one more thing to your plate? Before you preemptively start rolling the credits on this book, may I suggest that learning new skills and forming new habits won't make a stressful season unbearable. It could actually make it doable. The knowledge and discipline you gain in certain areas will free up time and energy. In that way, sharpening a home skill can have a snowballing effect. Every time you create purpose and order in one trouble spot, you can then give more focused attention to the next.

If you're drowning right now, please know that you won't be able to overhaul your entire life today. But you can overhaul something. So start by being a learner. Be a rookie. Have you ever wanted to learn to mend, braid your daughter's hair in creative ways, memorize the books of the Bible, or invest in the stock market? Improving in any of these tasks could reap enormous dividends in the long run.

Learning new skills and forming new habits won't make a stressful season unbearable. It could actually make it doable.

Each year, I make it a goal to learn one new practical skill or improve on one I already possess. I read a book, watch a series of YouTube videos, ask questions of others, and set a goal to become relatively proficient in that particular ability by the same date next year. I honor the commitment I made to myself by practicing, failing, and practicing again for an entire year. Practice won't necessarily make perfect, but it will always make progress.

As I learn and gain confidence, I find that I alleviate much of my frustration surrounding that topic, free up part of my budget when I no longer have to hire someone else to tackle that task, gain back much-needed time when I can do things faster or with more efficiency than before, and often ignite some renewed vision and passion for the work at hand.

Last year, after months of mounting resentment over my never-ending laundry pile, I resolved to make changes. At forty-three, I knew *how* to do laundry: throw the dirties into the machine, toss in detergent, press a few buttons, and let the water do the work—*ad nauseam* until the end of time. But with seven people, each of us doing one to two loads a day, we still couldn't seem to keep up with the avalanching piles. Each week, my towels formed an unpleasant musk that wouldn't go away no matter how hot I ran the cycle. No amount of elbow grease could remove the grass-stain build-up on my son's baseball pants. There was not one actually white tank top among my vast collection of white tank tops. They all fell somewhere between off-white and light grey on the spectrum. Laundry was my arch nemesis, my kryptonite.

I had been taught the basics of laundry by my mother, who learned it from her mother, who, no doubt, learned it from her mother. Often, that kind of generational passing down is all that is required for fundamental life skills. But technology and resources change the landscape so much with certain home-keeping tasks that old ways are not only counterproductive but also calamitous. Regarding laundry, I was sorting, washing, drying, and folding my laundry like my great-grandmother, and yet, her clothes were most likely not made of the same materials, colored with the same types of dye, nor created with the same silhouettes as mine. My washing machine was undoubtedly more advanced than my great-grandmother's, and, for better or worse, the twenty-first-century detergents I used were made with vastly different ingredients from those available in her day.

These reasons, coupled with a heaping dose of desperation, prompted me to learn a few new laundry room tricks. So I read a book. Even though it was entirely about washing and drying clothes, it was quite an entertaining read. More importantly, it convinced me to make a few tweaks to my regular routine that made a noticeable difference almost immediately. I was able to pass my newfound knowledge on to my husband and children, who carry their share of the load. Together, we've shaved off hours of work each month, have saved a significant chunk of change on our water bill, and have cleaner, better-smelling clothes than ever before. By investing enough time to hone one practical skill, I have earned back not just my sanity but also a small bit of life. This year, instead of spending so many moments digging myself out of my laundry pile, I've been able to turn my attention to better things.

First, though, I had to be a beginner. I had to be curious. I had to be an observer. I had to be willing to try new things with my laundry, even if that meant failing miserably at times. (If we're keeping score, I'm now the proud owner of a doll-sized wool sweater whose tag reads women's medium.) Whenever I misfired, I began again. Don't skip over that last part. It's the *beginning again* that matters most. You have to be bad at something for a while to get good at it. (I'm not sure how many times I have to make a cheesecake before it doesn't crack in the middle. But I know it's not seventeen. Maybe it will be eighteen. But even if it isn't, I'm certain my stomach won't complain.)

Don't despise your ignorance. Welcome it. You have to allow yourself to not know. As a beginner, you have to welcome uncertainties. Naivete can make you brave in ways you won't ever be again the moment you've done the thing and know what to be afraid of. You can't rush the process of learning or skip over the *in-between*. Yes, you will make mistakes. But failing at something doesn't mean *you* are a failure. It just means that you're making progress. It means that, like Adam and Eve before they ate that fateful bite of fruit, you are not just maintaining what is; you are cultivating what *can be* through growth.

> **Don't despise your ignorance. Welcome it. As a beginner, you have to welcome uncertainties. Naivete can make you brave.**

Perhaps you've heard of the ten-thousand hours theory, the notion that it takes approximately ten thousand hours of practice at something to become an expert at it. Psychologists continue to debate the accuracy of that concept. Still, anecdotal evidence in my own life shows that while continued practice may not lead to mastery every time, it often has a profound impact on the amount of joy I feel doing a task. At first, performing a new skill feels laborious. I make missteps. I'm awkward. The task is arduous. But, as I practice and gain knowledge, I improve in small ways. Improvement creates ease, which leads to something akin to joy in most cases. I still don't love doing laundry, but I no longer hate it—and that's saying something.

Is an area in your life creating too many negative feelings? Are there home skills that persistently command more of your time than they probably should? Have you been curious about learning how to do something you would typically outsource to others?

Beware the Lure of Tomorrow

If you're not sure how to answer those questions, don't try to dig all the way down to the root of your overwhelm. For now, look one inch below the surface of your frustration and start there. Turn your feelings of shame into curiosity. What skill or activity have you talked about wanting to try? What part of your home, your life, your work feels like a pebble in your shoe?

Maybe for you, it is the stockpile of junk mail, school forms, and kid's art projects currently spread over half your dining room table. You know you need to grit your teeth and tackle the clutter, but you've let the problem fester for too long, and now it might take a small excavator to burrow through the heap. Perhaps it's the nagging "I'm hungry" groan you hear every afternoon. Your children stand around the kitchen like baby birds with their mouths agape while you scramble to defrost the meat you forgot to take out of the freezer the night before. Possibly it's the pyramid of abandoned shoes congesting the entryway of your tiny home. You'd like to be able to enter or exit without wincing all the time, but you're not sure how to restore order in your limited space.

If you're anything like me, you overate the difficulty of whatever task you're avoiding. You fall prey to affective forecasting. You convince yourself you'll feel better about the task tomorrow than you do right now, and so you procrastinate for one more day. Most jobs, however, are never as grueling as we assume they'll be once we finally start tackling them. So just start. You don't have to wait until January 1 to make a change. Arbitrary start dates won't ensure longevity or success.

Be brave and take actionable steps toward a goal, or you will never see the finish line. Begin by naming the problem.

I need to pack up our house by our end-of-the-month moving date.

I need to organize my home library bookshelves so that I can find the book I'm looking for more easily.

I need to make two hundred cupcakes for the school bake sale by the end of the week.

Next, clarify your end date. If the project doesn't have a deadline, create one. Be kind to yourself. Unrealistic self-imposed goalposts will only lead to defeat. Then reverse engineer the project with your due date in mind. Let's practice this process by using one of the examples I've already listed.

> **Be brave and take actionable steps toward a goal, or you will never see the finish line.**

Say you've accepted a purchase agreement on your current home. You're excited to move into something that better fits your growing family but are anxious about the closing date, which is only one month away. That doesn't leave you much time to box up the ten years' worth of life that you lived there. But with some simple math calculations and some elbow grease, it can be done.

Before rolling up your sleeves and getting to work, you must first determine an order of operations. Consider the following questions in light of the job at hand.

- Is there one part of the task that requires more urgency and frequency or is more important than the others?
- Is one portion's completion dependent upon another's?
- Does there appear to be any natural or logical ways to divide the big thing into smaller, more manageable chunks?
- Would tackling a certain section or step first be more efficient or require less effort upfront than beginning with a different section or step?

Your answers will help you decide the order in which you should work. When packing a house, for instance, the rooms become natural dividers, helping you break the large job into smaller pieces. Your home may include a kitchen, dining room, living room, master bedroom, master bath and closet, toddler's bedroom, tween's bedroom, kids' bathroom, guest bath and linen closet, office, and garage for a total of, say, eleven smaller chunks or sections. I like my math to be simple, so if this were my moving project, I'd tack on one more phantom "section" to make it an even twelve. Your deadline dictates that you have one month, essentially four weeks, to pack. So divide your twelve sections (rooms of your house) by four weeks to get three. That means you'll need to pack up three rooms each week to meet your goal.

Accounting for much-needed Sabbath rest, you will have six days to pack each week. If you devote two days per room to packing up everything but what you absolutely need in order to function daily, you will be able to box up your entire house by the fourth week and still have two extra days (the phantom section) to pack those last remaining necessary items you reserved for the end, like hygiene products, a few sets of clothes, and kitchen essentials.

Here's where you may also want to consider *frequency* and *importance*. Chances are, you don't use each room with the same regularity. So begin by packing the rooms that are the least lived in, like the guest bathroom and linen closet, and leave rooms that are more consequential, like your bedroom and the kitchen, for the end. That way, you'll have access to the items you use most often for as long as possible.

Even when your tasks are not as large or spatially specific as boxing up a home, determining an order of operations can still be helpful. Namely, if you are reorganizing your home library to make it easier to find a particular book when you need it, you'll probably want to sequence your work according to dependency. Separate the books into genres before alphabetizing by title or author's last name because the latter grouping is obviously dependent upon the former.

Begin where you are. Begin right now. Don't get paralyzed by perfection.

If, instead, you are making two hundred cupcakes for a bake sale, you may want to prioritize your work order according to efficiency, creating an assembly line in your kitchen. Rather than mixing, baking, and frosting a dozen cupcakes at a time, mix up the dough for all two hundred, bake all two hundred, and then frost all two hundred.

Begin where you are. Begin right now. Don't get paralyzed by perfection. You've determined a deadline, you've broken the big thing into smaller pieces, and you've resolved to tackle the tasks in a sensible order. Now, it's time to put some sweat equity into the work.

Brace yourself against the winds of daily circumstances and distractions that will no doubt threaten to blow you off course. Begin imperfectly, but just begin. Imperfect progress is better than perfect plans that never happen at all. As Proverbs 14:23 says, "In all toil there is profit, but mere talk tends only to poverty." Any ideal circumstance you're waiting for doesn't exist.

The good news is that you can resolve to make a small movement on a big goal right now. Start by writing one sentence, doing one sit-up, deleting one photo, calling one contact, or paying off one debt. Start today. Then repeat that same baby step tomorrow. In the moment, your efforts will feel futile. But remember, if you read twenty pages a day, you'll read thirty books by year's end. If you save $10 a day, you'll pile $3,650 in your bank account by December 31. If you jog one mile a day, you'll log 365 miles in twelve months.

The Power of Small Wins

Sometimes, the difference between the life you have and the life you want is in five minutes. Like anyone, you have cracks of time here and there to spend how you wish—unscheduled moments that appear between one big responsibility and the next. While five minutes doesn't seem like a lot of time, three hundred seconds is the secret to a well-oiled day. When used effectively, five-minute habits can add up to big things by the end of the week, month, and year.

In the last decade, I've chipped away at larger jobs and accomplished minor, often forgotten tasks to free up more time for myself and my big dreams just by learning to better manage five minutes. By thinking ahead and creating a queue of fringe-moment tasks in the batter's box, I don't squander that available time trying to think of how best to use it.

Here are some useful five-minute power tasks that may help you squeeze the most out of any extra time in your day.

Pray.

Read a chapter of the Bible.

Make a list of three to five easy, crowd-pleasing meals and their essential ingredients. Place this list where you'll be able to access it on a busy week.

Walk around one room in your house with a trash bag. Collect things to throw away and/or donate.

Clean out your purse or diaper bag.

Look through a cookbook and mark a couple of new recipes to try in the coming week.

Read a chapter of a book.

Sort/answer the mail.

Fill out a school form.

Put one load of laundry in the washer/dryer.

Pull out freezer ingredients for the evening's meal.

Chop or marinate dinner ingredients.

Write a love note to a spouse, child, or friend.

Return a phone call/make an appointment.

Strip/replace the sheets and pillowcases from a bed.

Write a verse on a sticky note or 3x5 card and place it somewhere strategic for daily encouragement.

Toss out old leftovers from the fridge.

Water your houseplants.

Sweep the front/back porch.

Unload the dishwasher.

Exercise or stretch.

Put meat in a crockpot for shredding and freezing for later. Even if it's not meant for today's meal, it will come in handy eventually.

Think of three things you're grateful for in the moment, and thank the Lord.

Test pens and markers in your school/office supply bin. Toss any that no longer work.

Declutter the top of your desk or nightstand.

Clean a few mirrors in the house.

Take a walk around the block.

Delete old contacts, unused apps, or unwanted photos from your phone.

Clean combs, brushes, and/or makeup brushes.[1]

Life is a collection of moments. Hollywood, with its obsession over "big reveals," may have you primed to presume that if you can't makeover your whole life, you may as well throw in the towel. But be careful not to undervalue slight pivots. Just as an archer only has to shift his arrow a fraction of an inch to change the entire direction of his shot, small intentional realignments in your day can make a surprising difference. Don't bother taking a chain saw to your overwhelm when a scalpel will do. Start small by learning new skills, fixing minor pain points, and using your fringe moments well. Doing so will build your muscles and prepare your resilience for sizeable or more critical concerns. As a bonus, you'll free up enough moments in your life to start living again. Every hard-won victory, no matter how seemingly insignificant, will encourage you to tackle not just your big jobs but your big dreams.

> *Don't bother taking a chain saw to your overwhelm when a scalpel will do. Start small.*

Things to Ponder

1. What home skill have you always wanted to learn?

2. Which of your current home skills could use some improvement or better efficiency? Which one is most often irritating to you?

3. What large task have you been putting off? Set an end date for yourself and then determine how you might reverse engineer the job.

4. Is there an obvious order of operations for the project? If so, how can you insert that order into your tentative timeline?

5. What personal dream have you set aside because you've convinced yourself it's *extra*? What small step could you take today to get closer to that goal?

6. Make a list of ten power tasks you can do in your fringe moments so the next time you have five bonus minutes, you can use them proactively.

Wisdom from God's Word

Proverbs 1:1–7
Proverbs 16:1–3
Ephesians 5:15–16

The Motherload: Cooking & Food Management

Learning to manage the kitchen better is about more than just putting food on the table. It's about nourishing your home. A few new kitchen habits can help you pay it forward to yourself on busy days. With little to no added stress, you can ensure food is on the table without resorting to expensive and often unhealthy takeout options.

Prep Food in Bulk

Set aside one to two hours a month to pre-cook bulk portions of meat such as ground beef, chicken, bacon, ground sausage, etc. Separate these into one-meal-sized quantities (about 2 cups) and freeze. Then, throughout the month, when a recipe calls for the addition of a particular kind of protein, you can use a package of pre-cooked meat to cut your prep time in half. For instance, once a month, I cook three whole chickens in a giant electric roaster, shred them, place the meat in a zipper bag, and then freeze all the bags. This allows me to whip up casseroles, soups, hot sandwiches, tacos, quesadillas, etc., in minutes while avoiding the additives in store-bought rotisserie chicken.

Cook Once; Eat Twice

On nights when you have more time to spend in the kitchen, consider doubling the recipe you picked for dinner. Make two family-sized portions. Serve one recipe's worth that evening, then freeze the rest for a night when you'd otherwise grab fast food or make a frozen pizza. Almost any recipe can be frozen, either in part or whole. Depending on what you're making, you can often mix the raw ingredients, separate the mixture into two dishes, bake one, and freeze the other to be baked later. Or you can fully bake both dishes, eat one, and freeze the other to be gently re-warmed when needed. Dishes that freeze and reheat well include:

Casseroles (Reserve sour cream or mayo to be added after the frozen dish has thawed.)
Soup
Pasta dishes
Pizza dough
The filling of hot shredded-meat sandwiches
Hot breakfast sandwiches
Waffles, pancakes, French toast
Homemade bread
Cookie dough

Prep Breakfast While Making Dinner

If you know in advance that you will need certain veggies chopped or meat cooked for breakfast, prep these the night before while you are cooking dinner or just after you've eaten dinner but before you clean up the kitchen. For example, if your dinner recipe calls for one chopped onion, chop two. Reserve the extra for omelets the next day. Or whip up the dough for a batch of muffins as your dinner is baking in the oven. After pulling out your dinner dish and while the oven is still hot, throw the muffins in to bake. Allow them to cool completely, then store them in an air-tight container until morning. Prepping for breakfast the night before will allow you to serve two homemade meals to your family while only cooking and cleaning up once.

Create a Fast Five List

Write a list of five quick-fix, weeknight dinners you can throw together in a pinch. Store the list with the corresponding recipes. Try to keep the pantry and freezer staples for these dishes in stock. The next time your evening takes an unexpected or chaotic turn, you'll be able to consult your list, pick one dish, and have dinner on the table in moments. I rotate my list of five seasonally to ensure that I'm more likely to have any required perishable items or produce on hand. (This is especially helpful during my sons' baseball season when I need to make a picnic-style dinner to bring to the ballpark at least twice a week.)

Store Food Efficiently

You can shave off kitchen prep time by storing food in a way that makes it easy to find, easy to inventory, and easy to thaw or reheat.

When freezing large amounts of meat, separate it into one-meal-sized portions and freeze flat if possible (i.e., use a rolling pin or your palm to press and flatten raw ground beef that you've placed in a zipper bag). Thin sleeves of meat will stack in your freezer efficiently and thaw faster than "chubs" or Styrofoam tray mounds.

Flash freeze breakfast leftovers like waffles, pancakes, French toast, or homemade McMuffins for a few minutes before storing them indefinitely in your freezer to be eaten on busy mornings. To do this, lay the fully cooked items on a tray, spacing them about half an inch apart. Place the tray in your freezer for about fifteen minutes to an hour, depending on the thickness of each leftover. Once the surface of each item is partially frozen, remove them all from the tray and toss them into a freezer bag to be stored collectively: pancakes with other pancakes, waffles with other waffles, and so on.

Flash-freezing helps prevent food from sticking together, eliminating the need for individually wrapping each meal portion. When you're reading to eat, take one item out of the freezer bag and pop it into the toaster or microwave to reheat.

Stock your pantry like a grocery store shelf, with similar items stacked in a row, placing the oldest dated items toward the front. When making your grocery list for the week, you'll be able to quickly see when you have five cans of one ingredient and only one can of another.

7

Move the Needle

Life is long if you know how to use it.

SENECA

I learned two specific things about overwhelm during the global pandemic of 2020. First, despite what they feel like in the moment, overwhelming seasons are usually short-lived. They have a definite beginning and a definite end. While it may have felt like the coronavirus was *The Neverending Story*, for most of us, it wasn't. We made it through. Second, I realized that not all overwhelm is the same. Even though our calendars had been swiped clean, leaving us with endless amounts of time and energy, that year, we all felt limp. We had too much to process. We were navigating too many new things. It's like we were expats in our very own lives trying to establish basic daily duties without knowing the language or the cultural nuances. Sometimes our overwhelm was circumstantial; other times, it was emotional. Without good routines for this "new normal," all we could do was let life happen and reap the consequences. Faith in Christ did not inoculate any of us against irresponsibility. Consequently, idleness spread nearly as fast as the virus.

If the pandemic taught us anything, it's that we don't need to have more time. We all had plenty of time. We needed to use our time more wisely. Now, on the other side of that macabre year, Proverbs 22:3 has taken on new meaning for me, "The prudent sees danger and hides himself, but the simple go on and suffer for it." The year 2020 taught me that creating rhythms is a way of hiding myself. Daily disciplines bring freedom. While I won't always see the potential trouble ahead (who could have predicted a national toilet paper shortage?), I can build good habits into my day so when catastrophes do happen, I'm not overburdened by inconsequential things in the middle of crisis management.

Daily disciplines bring freedom.

Create Rhythms

The average adult makes upward of 35,000 remotely conscious decisions a day.[1] Most of these aren't life-altering or world-changing. They are run-of-the-mill choices of little significance. *Do I want to eat cereal or eggs for breakfast? And if eggs, do I want them fried or scrambled? Which blouse looks better with these jeans—the navy boatneck or the cream button-up? Should I answer that text with a heart or a thumbs-up emoji?*

In 2006, a Duke University researcher reiterated this theory and suggested that more than 40 percent of the decisions we make each day are so uncomplicated and habitual they can practically be made on autopilot.[2] This means that for nearly half of your day, your brain is often thinking about one thing while your body is doing something completely different. What if you could automate those decisions with intention? What if instead of making so many trivial daily choices and depleting your mind of necessary energy reserves, you established a few routines and rhythms for that 40 percent so you could stay highly focused on the other 60 percent?

We serve a God of order. Since we were made in His image, we have everything we need to organize our days. If you're a creative, right-brained mom, the very thought of forming good habits and routines might make you feel like you want to cry *uncle*. Artists don't generally like to be bossed around by a schedule. But trust me, freedom to go with the flow is actually bondage. Unpredictable living makes you a slave to chaos. You may think that you can't live an orderly life as an imaginative or innovative person. But that's not true. You just need to find a few habits that will work for you.

A good habit acts like a trellis. You can hook your time to it, allowing your days to grow strong and straight. You can concentrate on healthy growth because you're not burdened by the weight of holding up the entire day. In that way, good habits foster creativity because they give you the freedom to explore rabbit trails, provide necessary safety nets, eliminate potential human error, and make every job more efficient and timely. The self-discipline of a habit is a way to care for those around you. When you're not squandering your time erratically, you can devote so much more of it to them.

> **Find a few habits that will work for you.**

A daily habit prevents you from borrowing time from your future self. You see, if you choose not to root your days in some simple rhythms and home management practices, assuming that the unmade bed, the unswept floor, or the dirty bathroom sink will only look like that again tomorrow, so why make the effort to set it right, know this: It will, in fact, look much worse because today's mess will combine with tomorrow's.

Building a good habit is like digging a well before you need it. In the words of eighteenth-century essayist and lexicographer Samuel Johnson, "It may be observed, in general, that the future is purchased by the present."[3] How can you be kind to your future self? What habits can you put in place today that will make it easier to walk into tomorrow without having to stumble? There's no one right answer. Your unique life will need unique daily practices. Perhaps a few suggestions can serve as a line of breadcrumbs leading you to routines that would fit snuggly into your life. For your consideration, the following is a list of habits that have served me well over the years:

I start my day the night before. I never go to bed with dishes in the sink or cluttered communal rooms. Instead, I reset my spaces so I don't feel behind before my feet even hit the floor in the morning. Who wants to wake up with yesterday's burdens to tend to? Additionally, I look over my planner to remind myself of any necessary appointments I have planned for the following day. I set out all the items I'll need for those particular commitments, including the clothes and shoes I hope to wear. I take a glance at my weekly menu plan and determine what, if anything, needs to be taken from the freezer and placed in the fridge to thaw in time for tomorrow's meals.

Try starting your day the night before.

My kids don't attend a traditional school, but if they did, this is when I would pack their lunches or encourage them to do so. And then I try to get to bed at a decent hour so I don't end up hitting snooze a million times the next morning or sleepwalking through the following afternoon.

I punctuate my day with an evening routine. By giving my night a few steady anchors, I pay it forward to my morning self.

I dress for the day I want to have. Granted, I work from home. Additionally, I keep my outside-the-home commitments to a minimum. Even so, I always get completely dressed—in real clothes, with shoes. Why? Because loungewear is for lounging—which is exactly what I want to do when I wear it. Flannel pants feel like a failure by hour four. I find that I'm so much more productive when I'm not dressed in clothes that could also pass as pajamas. I value my work enough to outwardly show up for it even if I never actually go anywhere.

I create block shifts for my days instead of an hour-by-hour schedule. Schedules always make me feel as if I'm writing my entire life with a permanent marker. They feel too rigid and unchangeable. Block shifts, on the other hand, allow me to write each day in pencil. They are structured enough to ensure an orderly use of my time while flexible enough to allow me to welcome the unplanned. Block shifts help me build humanity into my days. To make a "shift," I divide my day into sections (or blocks) of time and assign specific tasks to each. Obviously, some of my activities need to happen at certain hours of the day, but many can be placed wherever they work best for me. My current shifts are

> Morning Shift: personal devotions, dress for my day, social media scheduling for work
> *Breakfast*
> Mid-Morning Shift: core subjects for homeschool, house chores
> *Lunch*
> Early Afternoon Shift: enrichment subjects for homeschool and extracurriculars
> Late Afternoon Shift: deep writing work
> *Dinner*
> Early Evening Shift: family time
> Late Evening Shift: reset the house, personal time with my husband, next day prep

I don't assign time slots to any of these blocks. Instead, I allow the natural transitions of mealtimes to create boundaries between each major shift. At the end of each time block, regardless of whether I've completed all that I had hoped to with those specific tasks, I reset my spaces (and my attitude whenever necessary) and head into the next block. In this way, even if I feel behind in one area of my life, I don't necessarily have to feel behind in everything. My time gets rebooted every few hours.

Naturally, there are days when the responsibilities of one block bleed into the next. My elderly neighbor might need a ride to the eye doctor in the middle of my mid-morning homeschool shift, or my high schooler might need help with a tricky algebra problem during my late-afternoon work shift. For the most part, though, I try to stick to the assigned tasks of each time block. Doing so allows me to give focused attention to what is right in front of me and get forward motion on all my responsibilities without letting one particular type of task rob time from all the rest.

Because I still have school-aged kids at home, I must rework my block shifts from year to year and season to season. The early, hand-holding days of motherhood necessitated a longer morning shift so I could get all my babies and toddlers fed and dressed. Now, surrounded by teens, I've extended my early-afternoon shift to accommodate taxiing to and from after-school activities. Additionally, come fall each year, I trade the casual, uncomplicated midmorning activities of summer for the structure that the school months demand.

I keep a running triage list throughout my day. When a random thought pops into my head like, "I can't forget to call Amy about dog-sitting this weekend," or "I have to remember to ask Jack to look for that lost library book when he comes home from youth group," I write it down on a running list of things I need to do, plan, or schedule for the day. While I could just tap a quick message to myself into a "notes" type app on my phone, I don't. I write it down—in ink. Not only does the physical act of writing by hand trigger the reticular activating system of the brain, solidifying the information in my short-term memory, but it also gives that idea a place. I can lay the thought down and walk away from it, knowing it will be there when I need it again. This prevents the natural brain drain that occurs with overthinking. Instead of carrying around an idea all day, persistently thinking about it so that I won't accidentally forget it, I put it in a container for safekeeping until I can revisit it at the appropriate shift.

I leave room for a "drive home" activity each weekday. When I was a teacher in the classroom, I had a fifteen-minute drive from work to home each day to unwind and reorient my attention. I could pull into the driveway feeling regrouped before facing home-keeping tasks. Now that I work from home, all my responsibilities overlap. I have to be intentional about choosing an activity each day to help me pivot my mind and emotions away from school and work to mothering and homemaking; otherwise, I can easily allow one area of my life to usurp another. During the warmer months of the year, I take a quick walk around the neighborhood right after my afternoon work time. In the winter, I typically make myself a cup of hot tea and select a podcast to listen to while preparing dinner.

When my kids were little, I wasn't homeschooling or working. My sanity, however, still required transitions, especially at the end of my husband's business day. I didn't want to greet him at the door acting like a caged raccoon. I wanted to provide a welcoming reentry for him. I wasn't trying to play the part of a Stepford wife. I simply wanted to feel like my own self again, not just a baby wrangler or a janitor. So, I brushed my hair, put on a fresh coat of lip gloss, and poured myself a glass of sweet tea. That simple afternoon liturgy helped me slough off the tension of my day and reset my attitude a bit.

Consistent Consistency

When things feel off-balance, we tend to grab for a better system—a planner with higher star rating, a new productivity hack, a fancy closet organizer. We're addicted to instant results and trust the empty promises of Instagram Reels. Ironically, these silver-bullet solutions usually require an exceptional amount of maintenance. They run on strict steps, overcomplicated procedures, and a generous amount of unicorn dreams. Perhaps comedian Simon Holland said it best when he declared, "No one is full of more false hope than a parent with a new chore chart."[4] Needless to say, flashy store-bought structures usually have the shelf life of a banana. In time, we grow disenchanted, toss our hands in the air in exasperation, and resign ourselves to the overwhelmed life.

But here's the thing: Constantly starting systems you never finish is just a busy form of idleness. Commitment with follow-through is a choice. Thankfully, you and I have a Helper, the Spirit of God, who can help us grow in the fruit of self-discipline. As we do, we'll feel the weight of responsibilities begin to lift, and we'll no longer give in to despair, feel impatient, or resort to unkindness. Even better, we'll be able to experience the other spiritual fruits of Galatians 5:22–23.

Your daily faithfulness in little things will matter much more and have a larger lifelong impact than your big one-time effort because consistency will always create more movement than intensity. An old German proverb puts it this way, "A steady drop will carve the stone." Your stewardship will make things better, not your perfection.

When beginning a new habit, it's helpful to pair it with an already existing one—a task you do routinely and at a specific time each day. This is called habit stacking. For instance, if you want to get better about taking daily vitamins and drinking more water so you can improve your overall health and ensure you have enough energy to tackle whatever assignments God gives you, peg those two small actions to something you already do daily,

Your stewardship will make things better, not your perfection.

like eating breakfast. Every morning after you eat, take your vitamins and drink eight ounces of water. In time, those actions will become associated in your mind, and you'll form a repetitive chain of events. You'll lather, rinse, and repeat the series until they become automatic.

In a landmark 2009 study on habit creation published in the *European Journal of Social Psychology*, researchers revealed that it takes most people eighteen to 254 days to develop a new routine, with the average person reportedly needing sixty-six days to incorporate a new habit into their daily rhythms.[5] That time frame can often be cut short by the simple act of tracking your habits. Since the early twentieth century, sociologists have been affirming what Luke 12:34 has declared all along: "For where your treasure is, there will your heart be also." When you pay attention, you prioritize. The very act of being observed changes the thing being observed. You will take greater care in how and how often you do a task when you begin keeping track of it. In time, your deliberate mindfulness and habitual affections will steer your desires. You may even begin to enjoy activities you used to dread simply because you're investing time and energy into them.

So track your habits, at least until they feel like routine. While you can print off any number of free fancy habit-tracking forms, you can also use a regular calendar. Every time you complete the activity, put an "X" over the date. Determine to be consistently consistent for at least sixty days. By then, you'll begin to notice you've built up muscle memory and have automated that area of your life.

Treat yourself as a friend, not a foe, by creating attainable goals. There's a reason why 92 percent of New Year's resolutions fail by February.[6] Usually, it's because they're not objective. The goals are too lofty or require large movements. Consequently, they quickly become burdensome. For instance, as I approached my fortieth birthday a few years ago,

I determined to get into shape. I bought a gym membership, a new pair of running shoes, and some aggressively bright athletic shorts with a stretchy waistband. While admirable, my goal was very ambiguous. What does "get into shape" even mean? *Round* is a shape. With little forethought, I headed to the gym. That first day, I spent over an hour working my way through the labyrinth of sophisticated resistance machines. I moved parts of my body that had experienced nearly two decades' worth of decline. And while the sudden release of cortisol gave me a fair amount of post-workout energy, by lunch, I felt like a human paperweight. Even my earlobes hurt.

The next day, I returned to the gym. To call my activity "exercise" would be quite generous. By day three, my muscles felt so stiff I was half-convinced that rigor mortis was setting in. Yet I would not yield. Belligerently, I soldiered on for a few more weeks. Because I didn't start out slowly, however, building endurance with consistency and care, I eventually gave up. I shoved my too-tight shorts into the back of my dresser, slamming the drawer shut with finality. Like a nonsense peddler, I convinced myself that exercise was too hard, so I didn't have to do it anymore. My unrealistic expectations and vague objectives doomed my outcome before I even began. I'm sure you can see that the exercise was not the problem. The habit I wanted to form was a good one. The way I went about it was my undoing. I was stubborn about my goals but not flexible with my methods. I clung to my plan of "getting in shape or else" like a sinking ship even after it started taking on water, was breaking apart in the middle, and had the word *Titanic* plastered on its side. I was not kind to myself.

Treat yourself as a friend, not a foe, by creating attainable goals.

Building habits requires discipline, not dictatorship. As you are practicing progress, trying to make certain tasks instinctive, remember to be realistic. If you've never read your Bible in the morning but want to establish a habit of reading a passage and praying for your family before your day officially begins, don't set your alarm for a predawn hour. Instead, soft launch. Tiptoe into the shallow end and slowly work your way to the deeper side of a commitment. Try getting up fifteen minutes earlier than usual for three or four days. Read and pray as much as you are able. Once you've managed to calibrate your body to that new schedule, set the alarm back an additional fifteen minutes, and so on, until you are waking up at your preferred time.

I'm happy to report that I eventually established a regular workout routine. I committed to intentionally moving my body in some fashion for twenty minutes at least four times a week for the entire year. My goal was SMART—Specific, Measurable, Achievable, Relevant, and Time-based.[7] By committing to a twenty-minute walk every day for a few weeks, I built up enough stamina to keep moving my body with greater and greater intensity. Now, three years later, I've logged over two hundred hours of Pilates, HIIT, and aerobic exercises. Am I saying I can do the resistance machines at the gym with ease? No, I am not. Am I saying that I always love my shape? Also, no. But I feel better, my clothes don't pinch, and most importantly, I made exercise a habitual part of my life.

The Currency of Attention

Progress toward my exercise goal took work. It took commitment. It took saying no to a thousand other things. It took the currency of attention. And that is the key, my friend. To claw your way out from under your overwhelm, you'll need laser focus.

Don't fall for the myth of multitasking. In his book *Deep Work*, author Cal Newport says that juggling between multiple activities doesn't just divide your effort; it subtracts your concentration, which in turn negates whatever gains you had hoped to make by doing more than one thing at a time. Referring to swinging from one task to another, he writes, "Your attention doesn't immediately follow—a residue of your attention remains stuck thinking about the original task."[8]

I realize the absurdity of telling a mom not to multitask. Moms are shape-shifters who change from chefs to doctors to librarians to janitors to traffic cops to judges to teachers to veterinarians to plumbers to electricians to dental hygienists to therapists to tailors to hostage negotiators and back again, all before breakfast. We play more parts than a one-man band. But whenever possible, try to reserve your deep work—the tasks that require focus—for times in the day when you aren't impersonating an octopus.

If your kids are little, finding the solitude and quiet to do brain-heavy work can be the most challenging. There are just certain projects that will always require greater concentration than you can give with preschoolers at your side. Obviously, nap time is a built-in pause to mothering responsibilities. But what about when your kids outgrow naps but are still too young to be left to their own pursuits? There's still hope. Institute a quiet rest time during your hour of pique productivity. Fill a basket with age-appropriate games, toys, picture books, and puzzles that can only be played with during these intense work times. (If you have a friend who could also use an hour of efficiency, consider trading filled baskets with her occasionally.) Strongly encourage (by this, I mean *require*) your kids to go to their rooms, lie down with a book, audiobook, or something from the basket, and rest.

Don't expect a child who has never had a "quiet hour" to sit angelically for an extended period just because you've said so. He won't. Like you, he'll need to be trained in a new habit. Start by explaining your expectations: *You get to have your own special time. You'll need to sit on your bed and stay there until I say you may get up. But here is a basket of things you may do while you wait.* Then, set a timer for ten minutes. If possible, use a visual timer to help a little one better understand what is required. Place him on his bed, hand him the basket, and invite him to explore its treasures. Walk away. When the timer goes off, return to his room and praise him long and loud for his obedience. Continue with this ten-minute routine for several days. Then, slowly add time in five or ten-minute increments until you've reached thirty minutes to an hour, depending upon the age and maturity of your child.

When I first implemented a "quiet hour," there was much weeping, wailing, and gnashing of teeth, most of which came from me, not the kids. To be honest, I got very little accomplished in those first few days. The deepest work demanded more than ten minutes of my attention. But in time, we all adjusted to the new routine and grew to anticipate the dedicated hour of quiet industry. Regardless of how much anarchy ensued the rest of the day, I could always count on at least one hour of single-tasking.

For the most part, I tried to keep this hour screen-free, for me and for them. But I'd be lying if I said I never employed the babysitting services of Mr. Rogers or Sesame Street. Listen, in an ideal world, screens wouldn't exist. But they do. So the question is, how might we use them proactively instead of reactively? How might we preemptively set screen times into the schedule to allow for our own quality work time so we don't have to resort to screens in frustration?

During the early years—sometime between kindergarten and third grade—I strategically allowed my children to watch a thirty-minute show at the same time each day. Like any repetitive action, it became a habit of our home. Giving them a definitive start and stop time ensured they wouldn't roll from one show right into the next and into the next.

Additionally, I planned that yes around a wholesome or educational program of my choosing so I didn't have to settle for whatever drivel was on when I started working. I used that time more productively than I would have if I hadn't planned it because I, too, knew the time was limited.

If you host a "quiet hour" or short screen session in your home, avoid checking emails, making phone calls, or getting distracted by social media during this time. Remember, *busy* is not the same thing as *productive*. Admittedly, all it takes to derail my work completely is a quick peek at my phone. Apparently, I'm not alone in this. According to a study by researchers from the University of California at Irvine, most people take an average of twenty-five minutes to get back on task after an interruption like a phone call or an email.[9] So keep this portion of the day short and strategic.

Busy *is not the same thing as* productive.

Getting It Done

Occasionally, however, the problem isn't finding a pocket of time to do purposeful work. Rather, the struggle is knowing what to do with the time you've been given. When you are saddled with many different types of stressors, all demanding your attention, it can be overwhelming to know how to prioritize them. Without a preemptive plan for how best to milk the most out of a quiet hour, you can easily squander those few precious moments in mental paralysis, deliberating instead of getting things done. Or you can focus so much time and attention on one particular project you leave other troublesome tasks in the lurch, allowing them to grow substantially more chaotic. I've been guilty of both, to be sure. Nevertheless, over the years, I've found the following four methods to be the most helpful for getting noticeable traction on all the different duties of my day. In their own unique ways, these four practices have been just the tools I needed to eat multiple elephants one bite at a time.

Big 5 List. Avoid writing a never-ending to-do list. "Do" can feel very oppressive, especially when you're already overwhelmed by all that needs to be done. Instead, keep to a list of five things—three timely tasks that need your attention today and can be accomplished in one sitting (like cleaning out the refrigerator after your six-year-old accidentally tipped the entire pitcher of sweet tea while reaching for the milk jug, or covering your tomato plants in preparation for an overnight frost) and two larger but less urgent projects that you can work on little bit by little bit (like going through one of the twenty-five stacks of old photos you've been given to create a slide show for your parents' fortieth wedding anniversary or piecing a few squares of the quilt you're making for your best friend's new baby). A Big 5 list will help you complete the most pressing tasks while also ensuring you get forward motion on larger, more meaningful work.

> **Avoid writing a never-ending to-do list.**

Loop schedule. You might have many things to do each week but not nearly enough time in a "quiet hour" or a shift schedule to do them. Upon closer scrutiny, however, you may see that your tasks don't all need to be done with the same regularity. This is especially true of house chores. Take cleaning the kitchen floor, for instance. Your tile might need to be swept and mopped, but does it need to be mopped as often as it is swept? Likely not. A loop schedule can help you create a chore rotation that prioritizes specific tasks (like sweeping) over others (like mopping), but guarantees that you'll eventually accomplish them all. To make a loop schedule, list out all the tasks for a specific type of work you'd like to assign to a chunk of time each day. For this example, let's focus our attention on house chores. Your list may include:

Sweep
Mop
Vacuum
Deep clean the bathroom
Dust
Wash the windows
Shake out the rugs
Clean the mirrors

Now give the tasks a weighted ratio. In this case, you might determine that for every three times you sweep the floor, you want to mop it. And for every two times you dust, you want to wash the windows. Create a list that reflects that ratio.

Dust
Sweep
Shake out the rugs
Sweep
Clean the mirrors
Vacuum
Dust
Sweep
Deep clean the bathroom
Wash the windows
Mop

This is your loop. Now, the next time you have a pocket of time to do a house chore, you start at the top of the list and work your way down it. Get as far as you can get in the time you've allowed for chores, completing as many tasks as you can. Then, make a mental note of where you need to start on the list tomorrow. If, for instance, you were able to dust, sweep, and shake out the rugs one day, you'd start by sweeping and then cleaning the mirrors the next time you had a chunk of time to clean the house. When you finally get to the bottom of the list, whether that takes a week, a month, or longer, you'll not only know you've done every chore on your list but also that you've given them an appropriately weighted amount of attention. You'd then loop back to the original activities by starting at the top of the list again.

One word of advice: No matter where you are in the process by the end of your work time each day, do your best to close that portion of the loop before moving on to something else. When doing a job, try not to leave the last part of the work undone. If your laundry is washed, dried, and folded, finish up by putting it away. If you've taken a tool or gadget from one room to be used for a short while in another, return it. If you don't put something back where it belongs, you may as well not even own it because you won't be able to find it when you need it the next time and will probably end up buying a new one.

Themed workdays. Another way to use one chunk of time to tackle multiple kinds of work is to assign a particular task to each day of the week. Like Ma Ingalls of the Little House books, who set up the simple weekly schedule of washing on Mondays, ironing on Tuesdays, mending on Wednesdays, and so on, you can create a no-frills routine to help you slowly chip away at multiple things. Caroline Ingalls didn't have an elaborate spreadsheet, an intuitive app, or a highly paid assistant. What she did have, however, was a routine and enough dedication to stick to it week in and week out. So instead of being frustrated when she couldn't permanently cross off "churn butter" or indefinitely check off "mend" from her list because these jobs were ongoing from one week to the next, she redefined what "done" looked like by staying faithful to each task on its assigned day.

Obviously, your modern-day hustle will look different from that of Ma Ingalls. But the system can be the same. If you only have one "quiet hour" to work, consider assigning a different task to that time each day. Because I have teens, I'm no longer limited to just one hour of concentrated work, but I still delegate themes to my days, especially in the summer when my schedule tends to need a bit more structure. Currently, my themes are:

Write on Mondays
Run errands on Tuesdays
Prep for homeschool co-op on Wednesdays
Write on Thursdays
Bake on Fridays
Clean on Saturdays
Rest on Sundays

Throughout the week, I keep a running list of small tasks that need to get done under each category. For instance, if, on a Thursday, I find a stack of books that need to be returned to the library, I don't rush out in a panic to deliver them. I add "library" to my Tuesday notes. Come Tuesday, I don't have to waste any time stuck in mental lethargy trying to remember where I need to go and what I need to do. I just consult my Tuesday list and get to it.

A few summers ago, to ensure that I set aside enough time each day to have intentional fun with my kids, I also began assigning a play theme to my days. Our summer play themes change from year to year, but they have often looked like this:

MOVE THE NEEDLE

Beach on Mondays
Library on Tuesdays
Friends over on Wednesdays
Park on Thursdays
Movie in the park on Friday
Hike on Saturday

Parallel play appointment. At times, there may be a task that requires extra accountability. You may have the wiggle room in your schedule and even the desire to do it, but when it comes time to put your hand on the plow, you procrastinate. This was the case when I began writing my second book. I had a message I desperately wanted to deliver, but since the deadline was still over a year away, everything else seemed far more important. *I need to create a better drainage system for my monstera plant, you say? I'm not sure how to do that, but watching all thirty of these YouTube videos should teach me what I need to know. I'll write a bit tomorrow. The Christmas cards need to be written? Never fear, I'm on it. It's technically only June, but you can never be too prepared for the holiday season. There's still plenty of time to reach my publishing deadline. The spices in the spice rack need to be alphabetized? I just did that yesterday, but it probably needs another once-over. First spices,* then *my book.* Before I knew it, I had squandered weeks of prime writing hours doing many nonessential things.

Then I discovered parallel play, a co-working structure designed to curb project procrastination. I sent out an appeal in a writing-themed Facebook group, asking if anyone would be willing to partner with me for an hour each weekday. I planned that we'd meet on a video app at the same time, check in with one another for the first two or three minutes detailing what we hoped to accomplish during that focused period, and then we'd mute our microphones and get down to business.

My partner would work on whatever project was most pressing for her—writing or otherwise—and I'd work on my book. At the hour's close, we'd unmute our mics and debrief, revealing what we had or had not accomplished.

My goal was not to collaborate on ideas or make a new friend. I wasn't looking for someone in the same season of life or who did the same type of writing as me. In fact, I really didn't care if she did any writing at all. If she had just wanted to have a dedicated time in the day to paint her nails, that would have been fine with me. My only criterion was that she be committed to meeting digitally daily and working side-by-side on something—anything.

That was nearly five years ago, and I've been partnering with a lovely mother of four named Kelly ever since. She lives three states away, is a part-time Latin teacher at a classical school, and, as an up-and-coming middle-grade fiction novelist and poet, has many long-range writing goals. Our one-hour commitment each day ensures that we both make wordsmithery a priority. It's a line item on the schedule. The partnership gives the time gravity. I'm less likely to fritter that hour away doing meaningless work or getting distracted by an outside-of-the-house commitment because the appointment holds me hostage. I don't want to be the one to rob Kelly of her much-needed writing time, and she doesn't want to be the one to rob me. So we show up, and we write. Should a friend call, asking if I want to meet her for coffee at that time, I can honestly say, "I'd love to, but I have a work meeting. Can we connect a bit later?" Should I have a heap of dishes sitting in the sink waiting for my attention, I can give it the side-eye with no guilt. The appointment gives my project the value it deserves.

Undeniably, it's difficult to chip away at a 50,000-word goal one hour at a time. The shortened span doesn't give me a long runway to get my thoughts in order. Over time, however, my brain has adjusted to this dramatic start-stop arrangement. I was not only able to complete *that* book, I moved on to another one. Since you're currently reading it, I'd say my parallel play experiment worked out well.

Perhaps you're not a writer whose editor is tapping her foot while watching the clock. It could be that you have tubs of baby clothes you're hoping to sort through before listing them on a consignment website. Maybe you have a collection of papers to fill out for your upcoming adoption. Possibly, you're a teacher who never seems to have enough hours in the day to grade stacks of assignments. It might be, though, that you just want to dedicate an hour to your own personal growth. You want to exercise, learn to play an instrument, work on a handcraft or hobby. Either way, partnering with another mom for an hour of parallel play could be precisely the accountability you need to make some headway.

Time is the most precious commodity of life. Remember, how you manage your time can be a reflection of your theology. When you feel overbooked and overwhelmed but are not actively doing anything to change what is in your power to change, you are not stewarding the talent of time that God has given you. "I want" is different from "I will." The former is a pipe dream. The latter is determination plus action. Thankfully, change doesn't have to happen in one large dose or with strenuous effort. Build your day around some good habits and stick with them. Don't waste your money on another overpriced planner or stylish storage solution. Just learn to better steward what you already have.

Things to Ponder

1. Take some time to examine the autopilot tasks in your life. Are you using those jobs to the fullest by being purposeful with your time investment?

2. Do you have particular habits that already help you have a more orderly day? If so, name them.

3. What is your typical response to unplanned, trivial activities that distract your attention? How might you design your day to be structured enough to focus on your priorities but flexible enough to allow you to respond to interruptions in a Christlike manner?

4. What is a SMART (Specific, Measurable, Achievable, Relevant, and Time-based) goal you can set today?

5. Which of the four productivity methods listed seems the most helpful for your current situation (Big 5 List, Loop Schedule, Themed Workdays, Parallel Play Appointment)? Brainstorm how you might best begin to implement one or two today.

Wisdom from God's Word

Proverbs 6:6–11
2 Corinthians 4:16–18
Ephesians 4:17–24

The Motherload: Cleaning & Organizing

Contrary to what Instagram might be trying to tell us, *organized* is not the same as *pretty*. In other words, that trendy but costly shelving unit you have in your online shopping cart might look eye-catching, but if it's not functional, creates more work for you, or doesn't pair well with your current lifestyle, it's not tenable and will only end up creating more clutter in the spaces you are trying to keep clean and organized. Instead of buying something new, consider trying one of these five ways to tidy your spaces with tools you probably already have on hand.

Communal Spaces First

Clean communal spaces first and in the proper order. When you are pressed for time and can't clean your entire house, focus on public areas, specifically the places you see when you first enter your home. Cleaning the main living spaces will help create an immediate sense of stability inside, even if the world outside seems to be crumbling. To do this, start by decluttering the area (see page 59 for The Motherload: Decluttering). Then commit to a certain level of daily upkeep or maintenance for that zone (see the Four Steps to a Fast Tidy I'm about to share). Finally, deep clean the space as needed, generally once a month or every season, depending upon the room and its uses.

Four Steps to a Fast Tidy

Tidying a room is not the same as cleaning a room. Tidying is up-keeping or maintaining the space daily and is essential to resetting or restoring order to your home. It's habitual. Begin by throwing away any trash. Then, put laundry wherever it needs to go. Deposit any dirty dishes in the sink or dishwasher to be washed later. By doing these three tasks first, you'll clear enough basic clutter from the room to make the rest of the seemingly overwhelming mess more manageable. Finally, sweep through the room, returning any other items to their rightful places.

Create a Procedures List for Common Chores

Consider making a written workflow for cleaning tasks in your home so you don't have to muddle your brain trying to remember each inconsequential step and so you can easily delegate those jobs to someone else whenever needed. By writing down all the necessary chores for each room in the order in which they should be completed, you can ensure that your ten-year-old dusts the dining room before he sweeps and mops it instead of the other way around. Write these procedure lists on 3x5 cards and place them with the cleaning supplies for each task. Be sure to walk through the chore precisely as you've written it on the card to guarantee the directions are clear and efficient before handing it off to someone else.

Organize by Type, Task, and Territory

Don't be afraid to ignore convention when using storage spaces. Just because the 1983 blueprints of your home designate the small alcove to the left of the guest bathroom as a "linen closet" doesn't mean it has to hold your towels and sheets. And just because most Americans place their cups and glasses in an upper cabinet near the dishwasher doesn't mean you can't place yours in a low drawer so your preschooler can serve himself more easily.

When storing items, consider *type*. Place like items with like items—pencils with pencils, pens with pens, markers with markers, etc.

Then, consider *task*. It might not look aesthetically pleasing to put your flour and sugar in the same cupboard as your hand mixer and favorite large bowl, but if you do a lot of baking and need to pull all those items out regularly, it may be best to store them together.

Last, consider *territory*. If your second-floor rooms have carpet and your first-floor rooms are all hardwood, store your vacuum in an upstairs bedroom closet instead of the downstairs broom closet. If you need the same type of cleaning supplies to clean two different spaces—like glass cleaner to clean the mirrors of two different bathrooms—purchase double the supplies and store them in both locations, so you'll always have them within reach wherever needed. In other words, organize in a way that makes sense to your life, even if your "organized" seems haphazard or illogical to everyone else.

8

Gather the Right People

Whoever walks with the wise becomes wise, but the companion of fools will suffer harm.
KING SOLOMON

There are two well-known lakes in the land of Israel: the Sea of Galilee and the Dead Sea. The Sea of Galilee has both an inflow and an outflow, which means it takes in the often polluted waters of the Jordan River but then filters out much of the contamination by circulating its contents onward. Because of this giving and receiving, the Sea of Galilee maintains a healthy ecosystem. Fish and plants thrive there because the water is always being reoxygenated. The Sea of Galilee nurtures life.[1]

The Dead Sea, on the other hand, has only inflow. It, too, is fed by the murky Jordan River but lacks an outlet for safely dumping impurities. The Dead Sea takes but never gives. As a result, the excess water has nowhere to go except up. It evaporates, leaving behind salt. As a result, the water stagnates and becomes saturated with saline. Nothing will grow. Nothing *can* grow. The water is dead.[2]

Like these two lakes, moms usually fall into either two-direction or one-direction camps: those willing to share their troubles with others and those who prefer to carry it all on their backs, alone. The former nurtures a thriving community of like-minded friends and family she can call upon for support and encouragement. The latter is so used to meeting the needs of others that she never wears *needy* well.

I'm not sure which of these two women you are, but it's worth mentioning that Scripture certainly never promises a special eternal reward for going it alone. On the contrary, it encourages every *me* to become a *we*. To provide a clear pattern for living under the lordship of Christ, the New Testament writers charged all believers to bear one another's burdens. They provided more than fifty communal imperatives to help the people of Christ reveal the love of Christ for the glory of Christ. By loving one another, building one another up, exhorting one another daily, confessing our sins to one another, and praying for one another, we can't help but take on the mind of Christ in tough times. We can't help but speak His words of truth in our overwhelming situations. We can't help but lavish His grace on ourselves and others. Simply put, how we "one another" with other Christ followers will directly impact our daily circumstances.

Made for Community

Woefully, our Western way leaves little room for communal care. We revere independence and individualism. We pride ourselves in our self-sufficiency and miss out on the comfort and cooperation of shared living. No wonder we feel like we're running on 3-percent battery. This hasn't always been the case and is not the norm everywhere. Across the globe and throughout American history, women were more familial and intergenerational than we are right now. They lived in small villages and rural settlements, rarely venturing beyond their places of birth. Single-family dwellings were the exception, not the rule. Homes included grandparents, aunts and uncles, cousins, and even friends. Folks gathered around wells, in town squares, or at the general store to share life and offer hands-and-feet care. Skills were passed on from one generation to another.

A natural but unfortunate byproduct of our wealth and industrial progress in modern America has been the breakdown of communities—of folks chatting over the backyard fence or playing checkers together on the porch. Once upon a time, when a woman hosted a baby shower for her best friend, she borrowed a punch bowl and extra serving trays from her neighbor. When her toddler developed a questionable-looking rash on his belly, she asked the advice of the elderly woman in her sewing circle. Scarcity forced women into face-to-face conversations. They couldn't help but invest in those around them and receive an investment in return. Now, instead, when confronted with a need, we turn to places like Walmart or WebMD. Our resources have contributed to our isolation. Because we own all the tools and have immediate information at our fingertips, we are less likely to involve our neighbors or friends. We don't ask for help because we don't need any help.

We lack community capital, and as a result, we've lost not only relationships but also social support. We're carrying the weight of the world all by ourselves. Autonomy may seem appealing, but it can leave a devastating impact on a life. Going it alone may mean you have no one looking over your shoulder, but it also means you have no one looking at you at all.

Online vs. Real-Life Mentors

It's not enough to gather people, however. You need to gather the *right* people. Christ desires the relationships of His followers to be built in and bolstered by the local church. All other places of discipleship and growth should complement a healthy body of believers. This is the accountability structure He has set up. This is the group He wants us to take our graces and grievances to so that we might receive godly counsel. In rejecting His plan for community and connection, we inadvertently reject Him.

Admittedly, the corporate church can be a hurtful place. Some of the deepest wounds can happen in the shadow of a steeple. (Ask me how I know.) But before you talk yourself out of submitting to the authority of a local congregation of Christ followers because of past wounds, you must remember there is no perfect church. If you ever find one, you best not set foot into it. The moment that you do, you will have ruined it. We're all imperfect people, being perfected by the work of the Spirit.

Autonomy may seem appealing, but it can leave a devastating impact.

At one time or another, we will all be hurt by our brothers and sisters in Christ—and, at one time or another, we'll be doing the hurting. But you cannot allow the brokenness of the body to deter you from gathering in Jesus' name. Luke 5:31–32 records Jesus saying, "Those who are well have no need of a physician, but those who are sick. I have not come to call the righteous but sinners to repentance." A church building is a hospital for healing, so we ought to expect to find it filled with folks needing repair. That's why we're gathered there in the first place. True, the four walls don't really matter. The church is a people, not a place. But that gathering has to happen somewhere. A cathedral, a living room, a meadow—wherever we are, there is the church.

If a real-life faith family is not possible for a short season, by all means, take advantage of the mentorship and sisterhood offered by blogs, podcasts, and social media. But know this: There is a difference between online and real-life counsel.

I was recently reminded of this myself while scrolling through

Instagram one afternoon. As often happens, a new-to-me account popped up in my feed. Whether attempting to matchmake or gatekeep, the social media algorithms had determined that this content creator and I would make a great pair. Based on my recent activity, the app thought I'd appreciate seeing a Reel from this homemaker announcing the launch of her $15 ebook about slow, intentional motherhood. *Why, yes,* I thought. *I would love to slow down and be more purposeful.* I clicked on the ad only to discover that its curator was a mom of one toddler who looked to be about eighteen months old.

I cannot fault a mom, young or otherwise, for wanting to support her family financially by selling products online. I also would never want to be guilty of disregarding the wisdom of 1 Timothy 4:12. This mother was setting a fine example "in speech, in conduct, in love, in faith, in purity." The ad made me wonder, however, how this influencer would encourage the mother whose nine-year-old woke up each night with debilitating bad dreams or the mom whose daughter was being bullied by other girls at school or the mom who just discovered her teenager's porn addiction. How would she inspire unhurried intentionality in those specific situations?

Contrary to current cultural belief, experience is not the final or only authority on an issue. We can embrace many universally accepted parenting ideas regardless of our acquaintance or exposure to them. (For instance, neither you nor I need to experiment with illicit drugs to know that they'd be harmful to us and our nursing babies.) However, we can both agree that experience usually leads to a certain level of expertise.

One quick peek at the tragic tale of King Rehoboam, found in 1 Kings 12:1–19, reminds us that the hard-won wisdom of seasoned mentors should require our greatest consideration. When deciding how best to rule and reign, the new king of Israel "abandoned the counsel that

151

the old men gave him and took counsel with the young men who had grown up with him and stood before him" (12:8). In his pride, Rehoboam foolishly followed the advice of his peers, causing a rebellion among the people and, ultimately, the division of the entire nation.

I knew nothing about the young mom on the other end of that particular Instagram Reel except for her obvious talent for making beautiful and emotionally compelling videos. I did not doubt her sincerity in wanting to encourage other mothers. But I couldn't help but feel a bit skeptical. Her fruit had not yet ripened. Her motherhood had not yet proofed. This was another example of our culture's obsession with style over substance.

As a woman who makes her living fostering an online community, I am frightened by how dramatically the landscape of motherhood has shifted in the last ten years. Young women now look to a screen to find their spiritual mentors, guides, and gurus. Yet while blogs and podcasts can have value and help point folks to the truth, we should all be wary of making them our sole mothering community. We should pay closer attention to the voices we are paying attention to!

The reality is you can select an online sisterhood just like you order a Happy Meal at McDonald's, picking and choosing according to your tastes—the admin of the Stay-at-Home-Mom-with-Two-Kids-and-a-German-Shepherd Facebook group or the host of the Single Moms of Triplets Podcast. By only linking arms with those who already agree with you or whose lives mirror your own, however, you're not actually investing in other women, but only in the agenda they hold to. You're creating an echo chamber, leaving little room for growth. You're gathering allies, not advisors.

Though it may seem that her life is an open book, an online mentor is more than likely only showing you what she wants you to see—the finished product, the completed goal, the happy ending. She can skip over the messy middle, the false starts, and the failures. She can tell you what she's doing without ever revealing what she's not getting done. She can leave out essential information whenever an exclusion might benefit her cause.

For example, several years ago, I stumbled upon a Facebook post by a popular Mommy Influencer. The photo showed the open trunk of her SUV and what appeared to be her weekly grocery haul. Hovering conspicuously in the foreground was her hand holding a receipt. The $60 total was not-so-subtly circled in red pen. "It is possible to feed your family for an entire week on a tight budget," she captioned. Not surprisingly, the comments section was flooded with questions.

"How?"
"Where do you shop?"
"What are your secrets? Show me your ways."

It didn't take long for curiosity to morph into comparison and eventually condemnation.

"Wow! My grocery bill is triple that each week."
"Why can't I ever find such great deals?"
"What am I doing wrong?"
"I'm such a failure at menu planning."

While I could certainly get on board with the idea of financial stewardship and doing one's best to stay within a budget when making purchases, groceries or otherwise, I also couldn't help but feel like her post wasn't telling the whole story. Because I had been following this woman online for a while, I knew a few things about her life that perhaps these other commenters did not. Weeks prior, in a completely unrelated Facebook message, she confessed to growing tired of playing Enforcer at mealtimes. From then on, she said, she would feed her two preschoolers half a peanut butter and jelly sandwich and baby carrots for lunch every day—the only two things they would eat. I also vaguely remembered her mentioning once that she and her husband weren't breakfast people and that they rarely deviated from their favorite dinner meal, grilled chicken breast with a side of steamed veggies.

In any other post, these personal facts would be inconsequential. But I'm sure you can see that by conveniently omitting them in the grocery shopping comment, this influencer was unintentionally creating social hysteria. If nothing else, the inclusion of these details would have helped her followers see their unique situations more clearly.

Personally, I'm a foodie who likes variety in my meal plan. I like cooking with whole foods, experimenting with ingredients, and introducing my family to the flavors of other regions and cultures. My husband loathes leftovers and cold sandwiches. Our four teenagers eat every meal like bears who just woke up from hibernation. We live in a part of the country with a very short growing season, which means that, at times, the price of fresh produce can be significantly higher here than the national average. In addition, we try to invite friends and neighbors to dinner at least once a week. For these and other reasons, my weekly grocery bill will always land in the triple digits.

Knowing more of that Facebook personality's story than just what she chose to reveal in one isolated post, I could walk away from her photo not feeling the least bit defeated or overwhelmed. I could see how different my circumstances were from hers. Unfortunately, most of the other commenters could not. In limiting her information, she was limiting their perspective.

But therein lies the clear difference between an online and a real-life mentor. The former can offer you friendliness. The latter can welcome you into a friendship. Mentorships operate best when built around relational reciprocation—the wins and the losses, the marvelous and the messy. If and when my favorite podcast host, YouTuber, or Christian influencer says something I disagree with, I might be able to ask a clarifying question, but I'm never guaranteed a reply. I can embrace their encouragement, but I can just as easily change the channel, unsubscribe, or keep scrolling when their words sting. I never have to stick around and resolve differences or restore what feels broken, nor do they. Real relationships, on the other hand, leave space for my disappointments, doubt, and even dissent. Real relationships offer me more than just commiseration; they offer community.

While I have learned much from the webinars, video sermons, and blogs I've enjoyed over the years, they pale in comparison to the sanctification I've experienced through the real-life mentors of my faith family. Why? Because online communities are microcultures that lack the fiber of flesh-and-bone relationships.

A life-giving faith family is one that offers a breadth of years, with women of all ages who can help meet your varied relational needs and be like iron sharpening you as you sharpen them. It consists of younger women looking to older women for wisdom and older women receiving the fresh perspective and revitalization of younger women. You and I need both in our lives. We need spiritual mentors, and we need to be spiritual mentors to others. This is our lineage of faith.

> **Real relationships offer me more than just commiseration; they offer community.**

Sadly, many older women feel unqualified, disconnected, and irrelevant. We overlook and pass them by, opting for newer models. And while it is helpful to reach across the aisle to grasp the hands of others in the messy middle of motherhood—women who, like you, are also raising kids native to social media and growing up in porn culture—you need to spend the majority of your energy clinging to the coattails of women nearer the finish line. You need the experience and encouragement of women willing to shout back to you that the way is windy, but it's worth it.

We need spiritual mentors, and we need to be spiritual mentors to others. This is our lineage of faith.

There is safety in numbers. In standing shoulder to shoulder with older women, you'll create a circle of bonus moms willing to fight on their knees for the hearts and minds of your kids. You can draw upon their life experiences to encourage and equip you for the steps ahead. These will be the women who will take your kids for the afternoon when you need to finish a big project, loan your daughter a black dress for her big recital so you don't have to spend time or money shopping for one, or text you when they're at the grocery store to see if you need any last-minute items for dinner.

Choose your confidants carefully. Guard against gossip and griping. When asking for emotional or physical support, do so before things spiral into crisis so other moms can lend a hand freely and on their own timetable, not out of guilt or coercion. Relationships will either help a situation or hurt it. Some women will fan the flame of your frustrations. They won't pray with or for you. They won't call you to change or grow.

So who is currently getting a louder volume in your life? Which women have you allowed to hold the mic? Are they displaying wise decisions in their own walk? Are they trustworthy, generous, and kind? Are they industrious and hardworking? Do they know where their value lies? Have they displayed a teachable heart? In my experience, women who refuse to be questioned often hide questionable choices behind closed doors. You don't need a release valve who just lets you vent. You need to surround yourself with women who will call you to do better, be better, love better, serve better, and fear God better.

Get Comfortable with Discomfort

You'll never find a model mentor, even in the local church. Sometimes, the best advisor is a composite of several conversations with many different people. More often than not, however, the perfect mentor is an imperfect one—a woman who doesn't have it all together but who is willing to allow God to turn her mess into a message. Be warned, though, biblical mentorship is a mixed bag. If you want encouragement to help you through your overwhelming situation, you must also be prepared to receive exhortation and even discipline at times.

> **Surround yourself with women who will call you to do better, be better, love better, serve better, and fear God better.**

In 1 Thessalonians 4:1, the apostle Paul urges (*exhorts*, as some translations suggest) the body to keep walking uprightly. He writes, "Finally, then, brothers, we ask and urge you in the Lord Jesus, that as you received from us how you ought to walk and to please God, just as you are doing, that you do so more and more." The Greek word for *urge* or *exhort* is *parakaleō*. It's the word used throughout the New Testament to describe the comfort that God extends to us and the comfort you and I are to extend to the rest of the body of Christ. But guess what? At times, it's also the word used to mean "admonish" and "teach."[3]

Sometimes, the comfort you need most in your overwhelming

situation is the kind that comes with the rebuke of someone who knows you intimately and desires the very best for you, even if that "best" feels unpleasant. Similar to resetting a bone, words that might seem like a painful blow can be the comfort needed to heal something broken. Exhortation can make a crooked thing straight to ensure health and growth.

No one ever wants to hear hard-good words—no one, especially not me. When someone has the audacity to give me unsolicited advice that could perhaps improve my circumstances, I almost always want to jump to offense. *How dare they tell me how to live my life!* Instead of receiving words of exhortation with open hands, I swallow them down like glass shredding my insides. Rather than evaluating the wisdom, validity, or scriptural merit of the other person's comment, I grow defensive and say things like, "Well, I'm just not wired that way," or "That's so outdated," and look for women who will roll their eyes right alongside me. More often than not, I'd rather stay stunted than continue to grow in excellence.

But suggestions about how I might best manage my time, love my husband, parent my children, or whatever (fill in the blank) don't have to leave me acting like a caged squirrel. Instead of feeling defensive, I can learn to be grateful that someone cares enough about me and my family to share the hard-good, uncomfortable comfort that will reset whatever feels broken.

Guard against hurt feelings when seeking counsel from a seasoned mom. Trust me, if you are looking for offense, you will find it every time. Our culture seems to have more triggers than an NRA convention. It is little wonder why we feel so frustrated with our lives. Even within the body of Christ, more and more believers are walking away from relationships, from congregations, and even from faith because we all feel emotionally wounded by others.

Someone upsets us, so we leave.
Someone offends us, so we cancel them.
Someone disagrees with us, so we return their rejection in greater volumes.
Someone hurts us, so we turn around and hurt them, saying, "I can't control how I feel."

Yet, in Christ, we have received all we need to control our feelings. Yes, you may be hurt, sad, or even angry about your situation and how others might view it or even how they view you. Those aren't "bad" feelings. Jesus felt all of these and more when He walked this earth. Feelings only become "bad" when used as an excuse to lash out, retaliate, or refuse the wisdom of mature counselors. They only become "bad" when you don't release them to the Spirit, asking Him to do in you what you can't seem to do on your own—welcome hard-good words even when they feel like bruises.

If you're going to be offended in a conversation with a mentor, be offended by your own sin of judgment, critical attitude, or fleshly responses. Genuine friendships can withstand disagreements, but not when built on the shifting sand of flattery or false unity. If an older woman always has to censor her words in order not to hurt your feelings, you've probably built a relationship with straw that will blow apart at the first conversation.

> **Genuine friendships can withstand disagreements.**

After nearly twenty years of sitting under the care and comfort of a spiritual mother, I can tell you that it's entirely possible that after the dust settles on their advice, you'll feel some level of discomfort and perhaps even guilt. Don't dismiss those feelings. They are not signs of failure but of growth. An unexamined life is a wasteful life. Sure, be shame-averse. Shame is a tool of the devil to get you to hide behind the bushes. But guilt and shame are not the same things. Guilt is the rightful check in your spirit that will show you how far removed you are from God and His ways. Guilt will reveal your idols, show you how you may or may not be stewarding your life well, and lead you to repentance and restoration whenever necessary. Shame will always lead you to defeat.[4]

Sisters in Christ are encouraged to motivate one another. We are to help sharpen each other in our work. Paul reiterated this in Hebrews 10:24–25 when he wrote, "And let us consider how to stir up one another to love and good works, not neglecting to meet together, as is the habit of some, but encouraging one another, and all the more as you see the Day drawing near."

Don't just gather people to partner with you in your moments of overwhelm, gather the right people.

It's obviously easier to reach for digital relationships, but if we settle for easy, that's the target we'll hit—every time. Instead, let's raise the bar and find value in the community God has given us, the local church. Let's be where our feet are. Let's be present with the mentors and other mothers we are with because these are the people and moments who can have the biggest impact on us right now. Together, we can turn the tide through teachability. Like the Sea of Galilee, we can accept both inflow and outflow for healthy growth. We can normalize the kind of humility that says, "Help! I can't do this by myself. I need you."

The tasks of motherhood may not always come naturally to us and may, at times, feel unmanageable, but with the hope of God's supernatural power and the help of the seasoned mothers He has placed around us, we can be "steadfast, immovable, always abounding in the work of the Lord, knowing that in the Lord [our] labor is not in vain" (1 Cor.

GATHER THE RIGHT PEOPLE

15:58). Don't just gather people to partner with you in your moments of overwhelm, gather the *right* people.

Things to Ponder

1. How comfortable do you feel asking for help from others?
2. Who are your confidants? Mentors?
3. Name three women you can call upon to provide physical, emotional, or spiritual help during a difficult season. Consider reaching out to them with a text or phone call. Ask them to pray with or for you regarding your current overwhelm.
4. Describe a time when another woman tangibly provided help for you or your family. What did she do that was helpful?
5. What is your typical response to another woman's hard-good exhortation? Begin to pray that God would soften your heart toward the wise counselors He has placed in your life.
6. Make a list of three to five ways someone could help you in this season. Share them with your trusted circle of women and invite them to share their lists with you.
7. If you are a seasoned mother, how might you come alongside a younger mom in her overwhelm this week?

Wisdom from God's Word

Proverbs 19:20
Hebrews 10:24–25
Titus 2

The Motherload: Holidays & Special Occasions

Birthdays, holidays, wedding anniversaries, and baby showers are supposed to be filled with memories and merry-making, and yet, to many moms, they can often feel more frenzied than festive. We are the "magic makers" of most events. We are the ones who plan the theme, send the invites, make the food, wrap the gifts, and set out the good dishes. Extraordinary days are filled with extras that can easily lead to feelings of overwhelm. Here are a few tips to streamline your efforts so that you, too, can enjoy all the special days.

Give Signature Gifts

Take the guesswork out of gift shopping by deciding in advance what meaningful gift you will always give for every baby shower, bridal shower, housewarming, etc., you are invited to. Whenever you find these items on sale, pick up a few of each and then stash them away until the next time you need to celebrate. A signature gift may be repetitive, but it can still be inspiring and intimate. With careful consideration, you can provide a meaningful representation of the most important things in life. Here are some examples:

- For baby showers, a collection of board books your children enjoyed when they were little
- For bridal showers, a pretty pie pan and pie server, along with a handwritten copy of a treasured family pie recipe

GATHER THE RIGHT PEOPLE

For weddings, a gift certificate to an "experience" the couple can enjoy together on their honeymoon or in their first year of marriage and a photo frame for displaying a photo of the adventure

For housewarmings, a clipping from your own garden, presented in a stylish new pot

Stock a Birthday Bin

Whenever you find toys, books, games, etc., on sale and within your gift-giving budget, grab several of each. The same goes for birthday cards, gift bags, and kid-themed wrapping paper. Stash these in a bin so you won't need to make a frantic, last-minute run to the store to buy a gift when your child is invited to a friend's birthday party. You can just pull an age-appropriate item from your stockpile, wrap it, and send it out the door with the partygoer. By buying items in bulk while on sale, you can set aside significantly less in your annual budget for gift-giving or spend the same amount but purchase higher-quality gifts than you'd otherwise be able to afford.

Determine Menu Traditions

If planning holiday traditions involving elaborate crafts and games feels overwhelming, skip them. Instead, use special holiday meals to establish the same unifying sense of belonging and generational connectedness. Determine a menu for each major and minor holiday. You don't have to plan anything fancy. Memories can be made around a plate of sandwiches or steak. Just be sure to serve whatever drinks, main dishes, sides, and desserts you choose for each holiday from year to year. If it's helpful, keep all your holiday recipes in a separate handmade cookbook, along with basic grocery shopping lists for each. Your children will begin to anticipate those meals even when they outgrow the desire to make crafts and play games. Because you must eat every day anyway, meal traditions can elevate even the simplest of special days. They can carry through to your grandchildren and your great-grandchildren without exhausting your time or energy.

Move the Finish Line

While some of the holiday hubbub has to happen on or around that particular day, the preparation doesn't usually have to. This is especially true during the Christmas season. While you may not be able to control the dates of your office party, the church cookie exchange, or your daughter's seasonal orchestral concert, you can control things like when you shop for gifts, write your Christmas cards, or decorate your home. Instead of seeing December 25 as the finish line, aim to have all your Christmas prep done by December 1. In doing so, you will make a very busy time of the year seem less crowded. You'll be more fully present at all the unmovable events because you won't feel the pressure and anxiety to complete the many tasks that *can* be moved.

Create a Christmas Gift–Giving Formula

Sometimes, the most overwhelming part of giving holiday gifts is deciding *what* to give. Instead of expelling extra brain energy each year trying to decide what to buy, put together a mental formula specific to all the major gift recipients in your life but general enough to be tweaked and repurposed from year to year. Yours will be unique to the needs and wants of your kids, but here is a peek at the formula I've been using for my children for years.

In their stockings:
- a new toothbrush with a fun theme
- a pack of gum
- a book
- a package of candy
- two "extra" items specific to that particular child's interests

Under the Christmas tree:
- Gold: a gift that is specific to their particular interests
- Frankincense: a gift that will build family togetherness
- Myrrh: a gift that will nurture their faith in Christ

I know many families who stick to a plan of "a gift you want, a gift you need, a gift to wear, a gift to read."

9

Let Them Go to Let Them Grow

Your home should be the antidote to stress, not the cause.
PETER WALSH

A few years ago, after felling centuries-old trees flanking our road to widen it, municipal employees planted white oak, hickory, and sugar maple saplings along the newly updated curb. The scrawny trees were presented like peace offerings to homeowners still grieved by the city's unilateral decision to level their lawns.

Landscaping a street with "baby" trees, or tree-lining, as it is called, requires an exceptional amount of tending. Regardless of how robust a sapling appears, transplant shock can devastate its roots, stunt its growth, and eventually kill a young tree before it even has a chance to adapt to its new environment. Knowing this, the work crews piled generous heaps of nutrient-rich soil and mulch around each base. Then, to protect the trees from the curious deer that roam freely in our neighborhood like a mob of docile street thugs, they wrapped every slim trunk with corrugated plastic tubing. Care was taken in the first few days and months to ensure healthy growth. City landscapers routinely dumped slow-releasing water bags along the curb to safeguard against dehydration. Wilting trees were quickly removed and replaced with do-overs. Our street was a continuous bustle of plant propagation.

But then, one day, all the overindulging and foliage-fussing stopped. With swift precision, a team of two sped down the road, gathering tubing and removing water bags. The trees, still so delicate and undeveloped, were left defenseless. The neighbors questioned whether the city's beautification project would survive the approaching winter. Most were confident that by spring's thaw, the street would be lined with dead trees.

The doubters were wrong. Six months later, after a typical season of harsh winds, subzero temperatures, and more than five feet of cumulative snowfall, a majority of the saplings were not only standing but beginning to bud. The landscapers knew what the neighborhood lay gardeners did not: Continued coddling impedes development. If the pampering had been prolonged, the slender trunks would not have been able to grow healthy root systems or the stress wood needed to withstand our severe Minnesota weather. The trees would have toppled before reaching adulthood. Turns out, some amount of pressure is required for plant maturation. The same can be said for children.

Micromanaging Your Way Toward Madness

According to the U.S. Department of Health and Human Services, childhood mortality rates in America have decreased tenfold since the 1930s.[1] Analysts attribute this significant jump in life expectancy to various factors, including breakthroughs in preventative and curative health care, advanced safety features in automobiles, improvements in urban infrastructure, stricter child labor laws, protective gear and team regulations in organized sports, and the widespread use of monitoring devices.[2] Put simply, there's never been a safer time to be a child in this country. And yet, we moms seem to be more anxious and obsessed about the safety of our kids than ever before. We treat them as fragile objects in need of vigilant surveillance. We build corrugated tubes of protection around them.

Gone are the days of two-wheel bicycle gangs roaming the neighborhood all summer, of sandlot baseball games after school, of moms hollering out the door, "Be back when the streetlights come on!" We monitor their every move, which adds waves of worry to our overwhelm. Instead of leaving room for the kind of boredom that breeds curiosity and ingenuity, we fill their schedules with clubs, lessons, and screens. Always screens. It stands to reason that if they sit safely at home with their eyes glued to a tablet or a phone, they will never encounter Stranger Danger in the alley. Right?

But here's the inconvenient truth no one likes to talk about: Our fears don't align with the facts. In a 2011 study, the Department of Justice observed that an estimated 105 children under the age of fifteen were victims of a "stereotypical kidnapping."[3] By 2019, there had been no change in rates.[4] In that same year, 156,502 kids of similar ages were injured and 1,129 were killed in traffic-related accidents.[5] With only a peripheral glance at the numbers, one could argue that driving a child to a controlled after-school activity with ever-present adult supervision has the potential to be measurably more dangerous than just letting him roam free. Unquestionably, there are numerous other variables at play in cases of missing children and car crashes that we can't disregard. Nonetheless, the numbers are striking.

I often wonder, though, if our desire to bubble wrap has more to do with our laziness than their safety. (Gulp. Yep, I wrote that.) It takes work, time, and energy to teach my child a skill I could do much faster, with less mess, and with more accuracy. But when I'm doing my job to train him in the proper use of a tool—ensuring that he is handling the instrument correctly, caring for it properly, and returning it to its rightful place—then I should have no fear in allowing him to use it.

Obviously, accidents will happen. They happen to me all the time. I'm forty-four years old and have decades of cooking experience. Yet just yesterday I cut my finger on the serrated side of a bread knife. For a few minutes, my kitchen looked like the intake tent of a field hospital. Who knew so much blood could spill from one tiny pinky? Some accidents are unavoidable, for me and for my kids. In trying to create a trauma-free environment for them, I am forgetting they are growing up in a fallen world where heartache and pain are a part of the deal of living.

This is not a parenting book, and I'm not a child psychologist. Still, it's worth mentioning that if you and I constantly micromanage our children, allowing their safety or our comfort to steer their upbringing, we not only add unnecessary work to our days by doing for them what they are fully capable of doing for themselves, but we also obstruct their growth toward maturity and adulthood. They have no opportunities to form fortitude, so, like over-coddled trees, they will surely topple at the first sign of difficulty.

Associate professor and director of clinical training in the psychology doctoral program at Long Island University-Post, Camilo Ortiz, has this to say about the lack of autonomy Americans give to their kids: "When parents hover and prevent children from independently exploring the world around them, they foster many of the processes that scientists have identified as causes of anxiety. Kids who don't practice independence (yes, it is a skill that withers without practice) are less self-confident, have worse social skills, are less tolerant of uncertainty, have worse problem-solving skills, and are less resilient. They overestimate danger, underestimate their own ability to handle problems, and catastrophize when things don't go as expected." In his opinion, kids need what he likes to call the four Ds in order for them to walk straight and tall into adulthood: discomfort, distress, disappointment, and (mild) danger.[6]

Put another way, your kids need to experience hardship. So do your best to curb the tendency to obsess over them. Quit solving all their problems. Don't intervene in every sibling squabble or resolve every relational setback. Yes, help them develop good habits and learn essential skills. Yes, teach them how to use real tools, even ones that seem somewhat dangerous. But then step back and allow them to face the natural consequences of their actions. If they forget something, don't immediately opt to go back for it. If they lose something, insist that they find it or replace it. If they break something, require them to repair or restore it. If they hurt someone's feelings, insist that they make amends.

> When children have no opportunities to form fortitude, like over-coddled trees they will surely topple at the first sign of difficulty.

Be warned, this kind of parenting is not for the faint of heart. I guarantee your child will make choices that will hurt or embarrass you. At times, he may even hurt or embarrass himself. He will no doubt act out of immaturity, sincere ignorance, or a desire to fit in with the crowd. But I bet you've done the same thing. No one is immune to foolish forgetfulness. No one is immunized from careless conduct. Mistakes are universal. How you handle his mistakes and allow him to learn from them will matter most.[7]

When your child stumbles and falls, move toward him, not away. Encourage him to make restitution, apologize, and take full ownership of the wrong before God and others. Dole out appropriate consequences whenever necessary. But then, hug him. Tell him that you still love him and are for him.

Don't try to diminish the discomfort or lessen the severity of natural consequences. Let the repercussions do their work. Whatever collateral damage your child must suffer because of his *right-now* choices will be less painful than the penance he might have to pay someday if he doesn't learn under the weight of his childhood decisions. But when he must stand and face the firing squad of retribution, stand with him.[8]

It's never too early to teach character. When my oldest was three, she learned a valuable lesson about honesty and integrity. While walking with me through the produce section of the grocery store one day, she plucked two grapes from a nearby cluster and popped them into her mouth.

"Maddie, did you eat two grapes from that fruit stand?" I calmly asked her.

"Yes, they looked yummy," she casually answered.

"That's called stealing, Maddie. When you take something that doesn't belong to you, you're stealing. And stealing is wrong. The Bible calls it a sin. Do you remember what we do when we know we've sinned?"

"Ask for forgiveness?" she questioned.

"That's right. We apologize to both God and the person we have wronged. Not only that, but when we steal, we return or replace what we've taken. Since you've already eaten the grapes and can't give them back, you'll have to pay for them."

Together, we walked to the nearest checkout line.

"I took two grapes, and Mommy says I have to pay for them." Her eyes filled with contrition, she reached into her over-glittered princess purse, pulled out a nickel—half of her life savings at that point—and handed it to a very confused-looking cashier. "I'm sorry I stold. I won't never do it again." And as far as I know, Maddie has kept her word, with grapes or otherwise.

Admittedly, it was a hard lesson to learn but an even harder one to teach. Everything in me wanted to overlook her childish action, forget it never happened, or simply add the entire cluster to my grocery bill. *Who hasn't snatched a grape or two from the grocery store?* But in doing so, I'd miss a valuable opportunity to disciple her heart. Did training and recompense take precious time out of my day? Absolutely. My entire shopping trip came to an ill-timed standstill. Did I feel awkward and uncomfortable at the register? Of course. So did my daughter. But the moral fortitude that began to grow in her because of her confession far outweighed any momentary discomfort she or I experienced because of it.

Now is always the right time to start loving your children enough to hold them accountable for their decisions. Now is the time for them to lose a game, stand up to a bully, disagree with a friend, earn a bad grade, or get kicked from the team. Now is the time for them to fail and be encouraged to try again. Now is the time for them to learn the lessons of real living—to gain confidence in their own capabilities. Let them go so that you can let them grow—if not for them, for you.

The Funnel Method

Undeniably, encouraging your children toward independence and trusting God with both their physical and spiritual safety takes a colossal amount of courage and faith, but the rewards are unequaled. Don't believe me? Just flip though the book of Daniel and look for the mother who raised him. Scripture never mentions her name. But I think if you lean in close enough, you'll hear it whispered on every page of his story.

> **Let them go so that you can let them grow— if not for them, for you.**

Overwhelmed Mom

When he was taken off to a foreign land, encouraged to worship foreign gods, and commanded to eat foreign meat, Daniel and his friends didn't just resolve to do right at that very moment. Obedience to God wasn't a new revelation to them. Long before that day, they had learned who God was and why He was worthy of their devotion. They had practiced daily faithfulness and spiritual maturity for years before they ever set foot in Babylon.

If you sit with the story long enough, you start to see what's not written on the page. Most likely, someone developed in them the strength of character and physical autonomy necessary to confront captivity with their faith intact. Someone had pointed them to the spiritual truths that would ready them to stand firm in a decaying culture. Someone had nurtured the resilience necessary for whatever fiery furnace or lions' den they would face. The Bible never tells us who that someone was, but I don't think it's too much of a stretch to picture a few mothers. I can only imagine all the hours of investment they poured into their sons from the moment each boy took his first raspy breath.

Recently, at an outdoor church picnic, I was asked to set up the refreshment table for our entire congregation. I naturally turned to my crew of helpers for help. A young mom of a toddler noticed my sons carrying ten-gallon jugs of lemonade and trays of cookies to the serving line for me.

"It's so nice to see teenagers volunteering. I can't wait until my son is old enough to help like that," she said.

"He is!" I replied. "If he is old enough to walk, he is old enough to help. He may not be able to lug an entire flat of water bottles," I said, pointing to the stacks of shrink-wrapped drinks my boys had started hauling, "but I bet he can carry one. If you establish a culture of capability in your home now, it will surely grow as he grows." Like Daniel's mother, that young mom had the power to equip her son to do great things, not just *someday* but right now.

The truth is that more responsibilities or larger rewards will be a teenager's downfall if he never learns obedience and stewardship in the early years. As Luke 16:10 says, "One who is faithful in a very little is also faithful in much, and one who is dishonest in a very little is also dishonest in much." That is to say, whatever you want your child to be able to do at fifteen, you have to start preparing him for it when he's five, and on the flip side, whatever behavior feels unpleasant at five will become unbearable at fifteen.

In that way, parenting is like using a funnel. When their children are little, many parents see training and discipleship as superfluous. They hold their "funnel" of influence right side up with the large opening at the top or start of childhood. They give their kids a long leash during the toddler and elementary years. They don't see a need for training in things like character, life skills, service, or resilience because their kids are little. Rules, boundaries, and expectations are set aside for "someday when they're older."

Later, in a sincere desire to help their tweens and teens grow in maturity and personal responsibility, those same parents begin to tighten the reins, laying down constricting rules and micromanaging behavior. The bottom half of the funnel—the latter years of parenting—becomes inhibiting and narrow. This approach often breeds bitterness and confusion in a teen's heart. Young people raised in this manner have trouble "adulting." They leave the nest feeling angry, cynical, and unprepared.

Other parents, however, decide to tip their "funnel" of influence and discipleship upside down from the start, beginning with the narrow end. They use the early years to focus on obedience. They train, supervise, and set firm boundaries to help their kids form habits of initiative and trustworthiness little bit by little bit. When their kids reach adolescence, these moms and dads then begin to parent from the bottom wider half of the funnel. They focus less on holding tight to a rule and more on building a relationship with their soon-to-be adult. Because the groundwork of character was laid early on, they can slowly release their tweens and teens to autonomy and independence. They do not need to control and superintend because their kids are capable.

No method or philosophy will ever be failproof on this side of heaven. Grand guarantees and perfect prescriptions are the stuff of infomercials. You and I are caring for people, not creating a product. Parents of special needs or strong-willed kids, especially, may require a vastly different approach than what can be summed up within a few short paragraphs here.

That said, nearly all kids are more resilient and able than we give them credit for. Small failures and wounds don't harm a child. Minor distress and discomfort can actually help him. It's through life's trials that he'll learn what he's made of—that life might be able to bend him, but like the saplings on my street that held fast through that first rough winter, it won't break him. The disappointments of childhood will give him a trial run to know how best to respond to the displeasures that are sure to come. As an adult, he'll be less likely to medicate his internal hurt through pills, booze, binge eating, overspending, or the like if he's been given small chances to practice holding pain appropriately.

Nearly all kids are more resilient and able than we give them credit for.

No conscientious parent would ever intentionally throw their child to the wolves, but in coddling them, we may unwittingly cripple our kids, rendering them easy prey for lions later. For instance, we create complicated "bucket lists" every summer to divert and distract our preschoolers so they stay proactively occupied through the season. As a result, they're never forced to manage their boredom until it turns to fascination, innovation, and wonder. We sell chocolate bars to our coworkers so our elementary-aged kids can meet the required quota for the soccer fundraiser. They're never challenged to speak articulately or practice money management skills by selling the candy on their own. We religiously check in with teachers to ensure our middle schoolers don't miss any assignments, and then they're never required to master time management and academic stewardship. We call places of employment when the bosses of our teens dare to give them bad performance reviews. Consequently, they're never taught to advocate for themselves professionally or build workplace integrity. Our kids never get a chance to fly if we always clip their wings.

Indulging children in their idleness or entitlement is not love. It is actually an unintended form of hate. In doing everything for them, we are not helping them to learn to do for themselves. Instead of working our way out of a job by slowly preparing them for launch, we are wearing ourselves slap out. Any architect will tell you that even a load-bearing wall will crumble if forced to hold up more than intended. The weight has to be distributed to other walls, perhaps not evenly, but certainly appropriately. Stop trying to carry everything for your kids. They can handle a little heavy lifting.

> **Stop trying to carry everything for your kids. They can handle a little heavy lifting.**

ResponsABILITIES

Of course, children will never grow to be responsible if they are not given responsibilities. Maturity is a muscle that gets strengthened with use. Home-keeping assignments are one small way to nurture personal ripening for them and practical relief for you.

Most people call them chores. I prefer *abilities*. Chores feel like work. They're done resentfully and often correspond to one-and-done tasks without connection or relevance to other, more difficult jobs. Abilities, on the other hand, create a culture of service in the home, provide kids with a sense of accomplishment, and teach them valuable life skills that will continue to improve and enhance over time. Perhaps it's just semantics, but in calling daily home duties *abilities* instead of *chores*, you and I subtly say, "You matter here. You are needed here. You are equipped and empowered. I trust you to do this well."

Maturity is a muscle that gets strengthened with use.

Certainly, chores seem like the most expedient way through. A chore is usually assigned with a swift, pointed command so that a home might quickly appear well-kept or feel less chaotic. An ability, on the other hand, necessitates slow and steady training. It requires a mom to think less about the current cleanliness of her home and more about her long-term discipleship goals.

When teaching an ability, I often set a focus for the month. Trusting that the task is age-appropriate, thirty days is usually enough time to follow the natural five steps of practical mentoring that lead to mastery as laid out in Syler Thomas's and Steven Tighe's book *Small-Group Leader's Quick Guide to (Almost) Everything*:

> I do. You watch.
> I do. You help.
> You do. I help.
> You do. I watch.
> You do. Someone else watches.[9]

When my oldest was in her early elementary years and learning basic home-keeping skills like washing the dishes, doing a load of laundry, and mopping a floor, I'd spend about a month teaching her a particular task. Once I saw she could manage all the steps on her own, I commissioned her to take over that duty for the whole year. At the end of that time, she had practiced to the point of mastery and could then turn to her closest sibling, my second-born, and teach him how to do it. They'd spend about a month being ability partners until he knew the basics and was ready to go solo. I'd then teach a new job to my daughter. I called this process the "stepping down" of our abilities. It was a simple, low-stress way of passing the baton of maturity that didn't require me to teach everything to everyone.

Stepping down skills allowed my older kids to mentor someone younger than themselves. They gained valuable leadership experience and made purposeful sibling connections that still continue today. As an added bonus, once my daughter hit her tween years, enough skills had been passed down that I no longer felt I was wilting like a neglected house plant. I had help—*real* help. There was naturally more harmony in our home because everyone was willing and able to play their own note. Granted, my house will never be photo-shoot-ready. *Better Homes & Gardens* won't come knocking any time soon. But I'm not interested in returning my rooms to "factory mode." I aim to inspire my kids today while equipping them for tomorrow.

Don't fret if you did not start teaching these abilities early on. It's never too late to instill practical life skills, even to teens and young adults. Golly, I only learned the most efficient way to cut an onion last year when a friend's teenage daughter gave me the same tutorial her line-cook boss had given her months earlier.

When training kids and teens in abilities, remember that your children cannot read your mind. You'll have to use your actual words, speak directly, and give clear instructions and expectations. You'll have to model the steps for them in the proper order, allow them to practice with your presence, and then be willing to inspect what you expect, providing encouragement and helpful feedback. But home care and cleaning tasks aren't the only responsibilities you'll need to pass on to your kids. You are raising future adults, after all.

Teens, especially, need to be nudged, not toward self-reliance necessarily, but toward God-reliance. This will require you to delegate other essential areas of life to them so they can learn to lean into Him in bigger and broader ways. In doing so, you'll force them to grow strong roots of personal and practical maturity while still under the greenhouse safety of your home. These are the years to start handing off the following:

You are raising future adults.

- Filling out forms
- Learning basic office programs/apps
- Making doctor appointments
- Finding a job outside your home
- Checking bags, passing through TSA, and navigating an airport
- Planning a menu and corresponding shopping list
- Cooking nutritious meals
- Practicing digital stewardship
- Performing basic first aid
- Managing a budget for day-to-day purchases
- Using basic banking skills
- Preparing taxes
- Navigating with a map or online app

Training in home-maintenance/trade skills (unclogging a toilet, turning off the water, resetting a tripped breaker, lighting a gas stove, etc.)

Learning basic auto upkeep and repair

Researching politicians, public servants, and ballot referendums

Please don't see this list as your ticket to the Misery Olympics or another anchor tying you down. Training your teens in practical skills and then expecting them to be capable of doing them teaches them that they are. What's more, the few moments it will take you on the front end to mentor them in each task will not only provide hours of freedom for you on the back end when you can gratefully pass the responsibility of completing those duties to them, but your efforts will also ensure that your teens don't leave your home acting like feral cats in a dark alley. Allowing them to practice discernment, make decisions, and advocate for themselves is a kindness you can give to your soon-to-be adults.

> *Allowing them to practice discernment, make decisions, and advocate for themselves is a kindness you can give to your soon-to-be adults.*

No More Cajoling

Now is probably a good time to mention that conformity and compliance are not the same as faithful obedience. A child who is doing a job while stomping his feet the entire time isn't really obeying. Similarly, a child who plasters on a smile and completes the task, all while inwardly seething, is also not genuinely obeying. Most of the time, obedience is less about an action and more about a heart posture.

With that in mind, beware the lure of sticker charts, candy jars, or other dangling carrots in your home, especially when teaching and training outward obedience and inward character. Sure, little treats are helpful in the short term to encourage preschoolers to use the potty or to motivate emerging readers to keep turning pages each week, but when employed to nurture things like honesty, stewardship, initiative, integrity, or hard work, they unintentionally tell a child two things:

> Your value is based on the outward benchmarks you can meet.
> You should make good choices and work steadfastly, but only when there's something in it for you.

Yes, commend him when he makes his bed or puts away his clean laundry of his own volition. Applaud him when he cleans up a mess without being asked. Praise him for sticking with a difficult task and seeing it to completion. Notice the growth that is happening in his heart and mind. Congratulate him for his effort, not just the outcome. But resist the urge to cajole obedience through bribery. Behavior modification tactics will always backfire. Like an addict chasing the thrill of that first hit, your kids will crave bigger and better prizes to put forth the same amount of effort as before. That feeling of entitlement will almost always birth manipulation and selfishness.

Two decades' worth of participation awards have produced adults who think that just doing the bare minimum should garner them a pay raise. They've learned that if they can't get a trophy, why even bother trying? Instead of showing up, they just quit.

Tickets, penny jars, gold stars, and tokens, while given with good intentions, are the subtle tools of legalism. Not only that, but they create complicated systems of measurement that moms have to maintain, which only adds to our overwhelm. Let's set the plastic incentives aside and find ways to encourage and equip without tally marks. Let's stop rewarding our kids for doing the simple tasks required for living. The sense of accomplishment they feel and the growing independence they experience can be rewarding enough.[10]

A Word about Allowance

But what about allowance? you may be asking. *If we remove outward stimulus, where does that leave allowance? Doesn't 2 Thessalonians 3:10–13 affirm the idea of compensation for a job well done? How will my child learn the value of earning a living? How will he learn proper money management and the principle of tithing?* These are all fair questions and ones I myself have wrestled with at times. But let me ask you this in return: Do you get paid to scrub your toilet or unload the dishwasher? Most likely not. Neither do I. These are jobs that must be done to keep the house functioning. As members of our family, each one of my kids plays an integral part of the household and must do his or her part to help keep it running. Completing necessary tasks around the house is a way to serve one another and steward the material things God has given us. Working together gives us all a mini picture of the "work it and keep it" command God gave in the garden, found in Genesis 2:15.

Additionally, if a child's general home-keeping abilities are tied to monetary rewards, what will happen the moment he gets an after-school job and begins to earn a small income? What will he do when he sees his allowance as dispensable? When the money he earns flipping burgers or bagging groceries far surpasses the few dollars he can get from Mom or Dad? In all likelihood, he'll stop doing his chores. He'll lack the incentive to work at home when the work outside the house is more financially fruitful.

This ought to compel us to stop treating kids like animatrons, shoving quarters at them to watch them go. Undeniably, hard work should be rewarded. You certainly wouldn't expect your local dentist to clean your teeth for free or your neighborhood sanitation crew to pick up your trash for the fun of it. However, allowance and compensation are two different things. Allowance is usually given for daily care and keeping tasks. Compensation is payment for above-and-beyond jobs—tasks that require strenuous effort or subcontracted labor. Hiring your child to do a larger, out-of-the-ordinary project and paying him accordingly is a simple way to teach the value of an earned income and provide the necessary money for him to begin to learn good financial stewardship and generous giving. So consider skipping allowance. Opt for compensation instead, which better reflects the work-reward ratio of real life.

Help for the Grumblers

It must be said that my kids don't always do their assigned tasks joyfully, expeditiously, or thoroughly the first time. Then again, neither do I. Sometimes I act like the commanding officer of a naval battleship during our communal home-keeping time, searching the horizon for clandestine activity instead of encouraging my kids in their efforts. Worse yet, I'm often guilty of judging my children by their actions or lack thereof while justifying my own mismanagement of tasks by my good intentions. Thankfully, these admissions are the exceptions and not the rule. But they are true, nonetheless. My kids are human. I am human. You and your children are human.

If my children refuse to help around the house like a bunch of draft dodgers or if they complete a task while unleashing a chorus of complaints, I'm compelled to do a little self-reflection. That's not to say I let them off the hook or I take sole blame for their choices, but I would be remiss if I did not admit that the sign of a good leader is one who can raise up other good leaders. As Mom, I set the tone. If I want them to serve their family without my prompting or prodding, I have to do the same. I have to model initiative. I must show them a Hebrews 13:7 blueprint by being a leader worth imitating.

When apathy or bad attitudes creep in, I can't return snark for snark. Instead, I pray that God will give them a willingness to work without complaint and that the fruit of the Spirit would grow in them richly. Only God can change a heart. No amount of finger-wagging will change the trajectory of an ill temper. I do my best to display good character, knowing that learning to have the right attitude about responsibilities also falls under the five steps of practical mentoring—I do, you watch; I do, you help; you do, I help; you do, I watch; you do, someone else watches.

Ultimately, I don't just *want* my kids to help around the house, I *need* them to. Expecting that they'll do their part is not abuse or neglect. It's not laziness or a deficiency on my part, either. It's an opportunity to help them grow both deep and wide. The "weather" of my home—the discomfort, distress, disappointments, and even mild dangers—will help to build solid defenses for them. Whatever responsibilities they are tasked with here will only make them more able out there. If the once-spindly white oak that now towers at the edge of my front walkway has taught me anything, it's that trees don't need nearly as much sheltering as I initially thought. More importantly, neither do kids. Overwhelmed Mom, stop holding up the weight of the world. Invite your kids to carry their share of the load. It's for their own good.

> *I don't just* **want** *my kids to help around the house, I* **need** *them to.*

Things to Ponder

1. In what ways do you feel you are perhaps overprotecting your children and impeding their growth?

2. Which of the two "funnels" of influence best reflects your parenting style? Have you seen either "funnel" method executed through adulthood in families you know? What positive or negative results have you witnessed?

3. What areas of home care or keeping are your children currently responsible for? What new areas might you begin to inspire and equip them to tackle?

4. What larger home tasks can you "hire" your kids to do so that they might earn an income, learn to manage money, and have opportunities to give generously?

5. Spend some time in self-reflection. Do your kids only hear you grumble and complain about your home or work responsibilities? Do they see you model initiative and a good work ethic?

Wisdom from God's Word

Deuteronomy 6:1–9

Proverbs 4:1–9

Ephesians 6:4

The Motherload: Miscellaneous Management

The more children you have, the more stuff you have to oversee and sustain. Maintaining complicated home-management systems for multiple people will only multiply your stress during an overwhelming season. Sometimes, the smallest tweaks to your home-keeping tasks can have the biggest impact on an overwhelming day. Here are five no-fuss routines to help with the everyday chaos of mothering many.

Color-Code Your Kids

Assign each of your kids a different color and purchase corresponding colored pens to represent them. Then, when adding activities to your digital or paper schedule, use the appropriate pen to record a particular child's time commitment. With a quick peek, you'll see who is involved in what ventures throughout the week. Additionally, consider purchasing everyday essentials like toothbrushes, water bottles, bath towels, etc., in those colors to eliminate the "It's not mine" or "It wasn't me" squabbles that can often happen at clean-up time.

Use Drink Bands

Purchase an assortment of colored rubber wristbands and store them near your glassware. If you've color-coded your kids, buy bands in those colors. Encourage each family member and guest to label their glass or cup by placing one of the bands around their drink for the day to prevent cup confusion.

Cut Food with a Pizza Cutter

When cutting large quantities of food for many little ones, especially menu items like pancakes, waffles, sandwiches, quesadillas, and pizza, skip the knife and fork. Use a pizza cutter instead to save time and energy.

Use Consumable Containers

Wash and save the empty disposable containers and packages of cottage cheese, sour cream, whipped topping, etc. Then, during acutely overwhelming seasons, don't pack lunches in expensive lunch pails and bento boxes that must be washed, dried, and kept track of. Instead, use the containers you've been storing. You and your kids can eat lunch and toss the lids and tubs into the nearest recycling bin. Additionally, use these same eat-and-toss containers when giving a meal to a friend or neighbor experiencing a difficult season. In doing so, you're ensuring that the blessing of a hot-and-ready meal doesn't later become a burden to the receiver, who must then wash and remember to return your more valuable dishes.

Make Each Bed Twice

When your kids are still in the bed-wetting phase or have become ill, double layer their bedding in this way: lay down a mattress protector, fitted sheet, mattress protector, and fitted sheet. Then, if they have an accident or vomit in the night, you can quickly remove the top sheet and protector, toss them into the washing machine, and head back to bed in minutes.

10

Loosen Your Grip

If a care is too small to be turned into a prayer, it is too small to be made into a burden.
CORRIE TEN BOOM

People are never as surprised or disappointed by my limits as I am. I'm a recovering efficiency addict. My natural instinct is to maximize each moment, wringing every possible drop of purpose out of my days. I want to do my work right. I want to do my work well. I don't want to squander even one second in the murky middle of mediocrity. But years of mortgaging my life on perfection have taught me that idolizing the ideal is not sustainable.

There is a difference between a Holy Spirit–led conviction of excellence and a human-made condemnation of perfection. Excellence seeks to honor God; perfection craves the approval of others. Be careful not to use your work to receive love or acceptance from those around you. That's work motivated by self. That's work propelled by pride. Don't try to be your own PR team, impressing onlookers with your capacity and ability to do above and beyond. Don't waste your full life scratching and clawing for social media hearts and likes. There is no such thing as perfect except Jesus, so don't stretch for what is out of your reach. Be willing to give yourself the same grace as you'd give a friend. If you are doing what He has called you to do, you don't need to defend the outcome. Focus on your obedience, and let God handle your reputation.

It's helpful to remember that while you are busy comparing your life to someone else's, assuming that it is so much better or easier than yours, there's someone else comparing herself to you and feeling the same way. You are in process. I am in process. We are all living in the already-but-not-yet of eternity. We're in the ellipsis. Neither one of us will be fully disciplined on this side of heaven. But, if God can be kind to us, surely we can be kind to us too. We can look at other women who've established order in their lives and refuse to label them "fake." And on the flip side, we can stop celebrating our chaos and calling it "real." We don't have to parade our mess, looking for applause. "Real" can look organized, clean, and calm.

If you are doing what He has called you to do, you don't need to defend the outcome. Focus on your obedience, and let God handle your reputation.

Sometimes, it's not the to-do list that is the problem, though. Often, it's the not-done list that causes the most anxiety and emotional stress. When that happens, we need to be willing to surrender the certainty of the perfect plan. Efficiency doesn't have to lead everything. We will never feel satisfied no matter how ordered our lives are. We will never check all the boxes. There will always be loose ends. That's just the nature of a sin-broken world. The struggles need not determine the course of the day. But how we respond to the struggles surely will.

Surrender the certainty of the perfect plan.

When you aim to steward your tasks with excellence, doing everything decently and in order (1 Cor. 14:40), you echo the steadfast dedication of the Creator, who always finishes what He starts. His commitment to completion should compel you toward your finish lines. However, your humanity should remind you that though you can be like God, you cannot *be* God. You have limits. You are restrained by flesh. Not all your tasks will be completed. Not all your conclusions will finish with remarkable flair. Sometimes, they'll just end *ordinarily*. Embracing that truth is not permission to throw in the towel, friend. It is an acknowledgment that God is *other*. You are not.

Learn to get comfortable with *good enough*, *imperfect*, or *for right now*. Every decision you make doesn't have to be so serious and demand so much from you. You are allowed to acknowledge the progress, even if it never wraps up perfectly. If you only ever focus on what is *not* getting completed, all the great things that you have done and are doing will go unnoticed. You'll forget to be grateful. You'll forget to praise the One who put those plans in motion and walked alongside you, orchestrating victory. You don't always have to be looking for the next hurdle to jump. You can be radical and revolutionary by not being so busy that you buckle. You can pause to celebrate the wins.

> **Be the mom who is easily delighted—the mom with an exceptionally low joy bar.**

Don't be embarrassed or ashamed to be the fun mom, the one who doesn't allow her tasks to have totalitarian rule over her days. Be the mom who is easily delighted—the mom with an exceptionally low joy bar. Look for pleasure in little things. Suck the marrow out of every miraculous moment, no matter how inconsequential. As you give more of your attention to the beauty right in front of you, the daily battles of life will begin to feel less burdensome.

Never Consumed

Here's a little secret I don't often admit, even to myself: I don't really want to need grace. Frankly, I don't usually trust that others will extend it to me. Maybe that's because I often find it difficult to extend it to them, especially when I'm overtaxed and overwhelmed. I want to be able to pull myself up, get it all down, and launch a five-part course about how to do it on Instagram before my head hits the pillow each night. A lifetime of watching movies with underdog heroes has conditioned me to believe I can do it all alone. And if, on the off chance, I need help from my husband or kids, I want it done my way or else.

Yet if my children never see me cast my burdens on others, especially the Lord, how will they learn to ask for help? How will they ever know to lean on Him? If I'm never vulnerable enough to admit my weaknesses and show them my reliance on a Savior, what will convince them they need one too?

You see, anything that brings you closer to God or makes you rely on Him more fully is a blessing, not a curse. Your overwhelm might feel like a millstone around your neck or perhaps even a punishment. But it's not. It's an invitation to dependence. After all, why would you ever reach for a Rescuer if you never needed rescuing? So be careful not to self-help your way out of every problem meant to draw you to the One who can help best. There's no scarcity with God, friend. He's in the business of multiplying—of making something out of nothing.

When you feel empty of your time, your energy, your resources, turn to Him. He always has more. One quick flip to 1 Kings 17:8–16 shows that the widow of Zarephath learned this firsthand. Because a drought had ravaged the land, she only had enough flour and oil to prepare one final meal. "I am gathering a couple of sticks that I may go in and prepare it for myself and my son, that we may eat it and die," she confessed to Elijah (17:12). This was more than just a dramatic declaration. This was the sound of surrender. This was a mother at the end of her hope, at the end of herself.

The prophet, however, was nonplussed. "'Do not fear; go and do as you have said. But first make me a little cake of it and bring it to me, and afterward make something for yourself and your son'" (17:13). Elijah gave the widow 1 Thessalonians 4:11–12 kind of advice. He told her to mind her business and work with her hands—to make loaves of bread. The widow was charged with faithfulness; God was charged with the results. Not surprisingly, He made good on His promise. Until He saw fit to send rain to replenish the parched earth, the Lord kept her larder full. The jar of flour never emptied, and the jug of oil never ran dry.

Why would you ever reach for a Rescuer if you never needed rescuing?

In 2022, while making tacos for dinner on some random Tuesday evening, I sent out a desperate plea to three of my friends. Between sobs, I poured out months of frustration and disappointment. So much of my life seemed to be spiraling. A few minutes later, however, after I recovered from my vulnerability hangover, I realized that my life wasn't spiraling—not really. Life was hard. Life was busy. At times, I felt incredibly ragged. But this was only an acute season of overwhelm. This was not an overwhelming life. And because I had all the tools necessary to keep the routine parts of my days going, I could be more clear-headed about the unexpected. Like the bread-baking widow, I would manage what I could and give the rest to God.

Be Still and Know

It's been two years since that fateful video plea. Since then, my stepdad passed away. I spent nearly a week packing up my mom's entire house and moving her across the country to be closer to family. Her memory continues to rapidly decline, forcing me to mourn the losses daily. Thanks to inflation, a small leak in our master bedroom ceiling cost $7,000 more than the original estimate to repair. I stood helplessly by as my mother and, not long after, my mother-in-law each received a devastating cancer diagnosis.

Combine all of that with the family parties I planned, the college forms I filled out, the women's ministry events I organized, the homeschool co-op I led, the meals I served, the laundry I folded, the errands I ran, the bills I paid, and you have the makings of a repeat performance of 2022. I should be writing to you from the fetal position, but I'm not. God has turned my sometimes tired and often unimpressive offerings into something meaningful. He has multiplied.

I just had to be willing to loosen my grip. I just had to be disciplined enough to leave things undone. As Psalm 46:10, says, I had to be still and know that He is God. Even on a busy day, even on my busiest day. *Still* here is *rāpâ* in Hebrew. It means to be feeble, to fail, to weaken. It means to drop. To let go.[1] Did you catch that? Being still requires that we unclench our fists—to open our hands, to cease striving. *Overwhelm* is sometimes a control issue. We want to do it our way. We want to do it by ourselves. Nevertheless, anytime we hold something too tightly, we usually end up strangling it. Or maybe that's just me.

When you feel ragged and worn thin, don't just do something; stand there. Be still. Jesus has already provided the blood and sweat, and I've no doubt you've poured out enough tears. So pray for order, pray for strength, pray for peace, and then let go. Like the widow, allow God to fill the jars and the jugs when you cannot. Trust His tender care. You'll be able to repeat the words of the psalmist David, who wrote, "Praise be to the Lord, to God our Savior, who daily bears our burdens" (Ps. 68:19 NIV). He's your certainty in the struggle.

Where Your Worth Comes From

So much of your mother-work is unseen. Changing diapers, picking up dirty towels from the bathroom floor, and sitting in the carpool lane until the end of time. You work in humble places. It's easy to feel undervalued and underappreciated, especially when you've been ground down by a steady stream of to-dos demanding your attention. But amid your toil, don't forget what Colossians 1:16 says: that God is at work creating the visible and the invisible. He is a God of hidden tasks too. He makes and sustains every breath we take, holds the galaxies up and keeps them turning, and swirls the sand beneath each wave. Though no one may ever see all He does, He's unceasing in His service.

When you feel ragged and worn thin, don't just do something; stand there. Be still.

Every time you quietly restore order to this broken world, laboring in the shadows of your home, you partner with the Lord. Your daily faithfulness is an act of worship that declares, "Though no one else sees, God, You do, and that is enough."

This is contrary to the message of the current go-get culture. The world says you are what you make. But don't confuse belongings for belonging. You are a human being, not a human doing. Mind you, there's nothing wrong with working hard. There's nothing wrong with wanting to leave a legacy. But if you really want to impact change, don't bother running for office, starting a blog, or leading a committee. Rather, have a great conversation with your child, spend time in the Word as a family, bring a bowl of soup to an ailing neighbor, look the barista in the eye and call her by name, or laugh with a friend. Live extraordinarily ordinary, and the effects of your influence will be felt for generations.

Your value is not calculated by how much you produce, how efficient you are, or how many tasks you can complete. Your worth comes from God. He's not impressed by your furrowed brow and calloused hands. He's not threatened or disappointed by your inabilities or fractured pieces. There's a difference between being willing to do anything for God and feeling like you need to do everything for Him.

The reality is, God's plans will be accomplished with or without you. In that way, you are insignificant but important. He doesn't need you in the work of raising children, keeping a home, and serving in the public square. But in His love, He chooses to use you. He welcomes you into the work He has for you. Isn't that freeing? If you let it, that realization can help unchain you from the shackles of guilt and defeat you may be feeling right now because of how much you have or have not accomplished today.

God hears the tears you cry in secret. He knows you are weary. He sees your daily investment and cares deeply about your desire to spend your life well. You are not forgotten. Though you may feel bruised, He will not let you break (Matt. 12:20). Remember, the God of the universe has already overcome. The winds and the waves still obey Him.

So take heart and stop trying so hard.

So take heart and stop trying so hard. Instead, lead a quiet life, mind your own business, and work with your hands. In that way, your overwhelm can be the canvas on which you paint your theology. The watching world will witness every brush stroke. So live in such a way that there is no explanation but Jesus.

Acknowledgments

When I set out to write a book about overwhelm in 2022, I had no idea I would do it during one of the most overwhelming seasons of my life. If I've learned anything in the last two years of throwing words at a page, it's that God will never give me a message to share that He doesn't first want me to live. In His unbelievable kindness, He sent just the right people to walk shoulder to shoulder with me every step of the way. Though, at times, I felt bent under the weight of the work, the following people ensured I never buckled.

Lauren Anderson, Rosita Anderson, Emily Homan, Shelby Huchthausen, Amy Johnson, Cori McCumsey, Jennifer Poole, and Jessica Winter, thank you for reading every word and for telling me the truth about all of them. France Walsh, thank you for saying yes to coffee even before I began writing this book and for saying no to reading the rough draft when it was done. Those two little words were more affirming than I'll ever be able to articulate. I appreciate your willingness to say both with boldness!

Keely Boeving, my agent, four years ago you encouraged me to write two books instead of just one, and it turns out you were right all along. I promise to listen the next time.

Judy Dunagan, I'm so grateful to have been in your expert hands once again. Thank you for holding my words with care and being the kind of Titus 2 mentor my writing needed. I'm cheering you on as you start your next chapter. Annette LaPlaca, thank you for smoothing out all the raw edges. Sometimes, you had to use a chainsaw; other times, a scalpel. You expertly wielded both. Kaylee Lockenour Dunn, Ashley Torres, Catherine Parks, Janis Backing, and the entire team at Moody Publishers, you have taken a green writer and helped her to grow. Thank you for nurturing not just these few words but also my future work.

Kelly Hellmuth, thanks for forcing my hand to the plow each and every afternoon, for writing your way and for letting me write mine. I'm glad we're partners. I'm honored we're friends.

Emily Gutenkauf, Sarah Ho, Lora Kesselhon, Amy Johnson, Shannon Pfeffer, and Jenny Roub, thank you so much for not blocking my number, for answering each frantic text with encouraging words, a heartfelt prayer, or a sarcastic meme, and for always knowing which of the three I needed most.

Maureen and Glen, you were such a support to me in the baby wrangling years. Thank you for never judging me when I fell asleep on your couch and for keeping everyone alive while I napped.

Mom, thank you for always clapping until your hands hurt. I know your life was overwhelming at times, and yet you never made me feel like I was the reason. I can narrate a good story about my kids because you taught me how.

Madeline, Reese, Finnlae, Jack, and Jude, out of all my names, *Mom* is my favorite. You are my most important work. Over the years, you've seen me in desperate need of rescuing. I hope you've also seen me clinging to the Rescuer.

Dain, there's no one I'd rather make tacos for than you. I promise not to cry every time I make them. Thank you for eating them anyway when I do. Most importantly, thank you for hearing the words I'm not brave enough to say.

Jesus, thank You for always being *everything* so that I never have to be.

Notes

Chapter 1: Mind Your Business

Epigraph: Lysa TerKeurst, *Good Boundaries and Goodbyes* (Nelson, 2022), 8.
1. "G2270 - hēsychazō - Strong's Greek Lexicon (KJV)," Blue Letter Bible, accessed October 11, 2024, https://www.blueletterbible.org/lexicon/g2270/kjv/tr/0-1/.

Chapter 2: Narrate a Good Story

Epigraph: Abbie Halberstadt, *Hard Is Not the Same Thing as Bad* (Harvest House, 2023), title page.
1. Patrícia Marzola et al., "Exploring the Role of Neuroplasticity in Development, Aging, and Neurodegeneration," *Brain Sciences* 13, no. 12 (2023): 1610, https://doi.org/10.3390/brainsci13121610.
2. Beacon MM, "Cognitive Behavioral Therapy and Neuroplasticity: How CBT Changes Your Brain," Lukin Center for Psychotherapy, accessed March 9, 2023, https://www.lukincenter.com/cognitive-behavioral-therapy-and-neuroplasticity-how-cbt-changes-your-brain/.
3. Jamie Erickson (@momtomompodcast), "Yesterday, one of my pastors mentioned that prayer is one way to acknowledge our dependence on God," Instagram, March 20, 2023, https://www.instagram.com/p/CqA0_tMrwqw/.

Chapter 3: Edit with Intention

Epigraph: Elisabeth Elliot, *A Lamp Unto My Feet* (Revell, 1985), 250, ebook.
1. Stacey Jo Dixon, "Number of Monthly Active Pinterest Users Worldwide From 1st Quarter 2016 to 3rd Quarter 2024," Statista, November 11, 2024, https://www.statista.com/statistics/463353/pinterest-global-mau.

2. Andrew Lipsman, "Why Facebook Provides Scale, but Instagram and Pinterest Offer Relevance for Social Commerce," Emarketer, June 5, 2019, https://www.emarketer.com/content/why-facebook-provides-scale-but-instagram-and-pinterest-offer-relevance-for-social-commerce.
3. "Are You Addicted to Your Phone? American Phone Usage & Screen Time Statistics," Harmony Healthcare IT, January 8, 2025, https://www.harmonyhit.com/phone-screen-time-statistics/.
4. Jonathan Swift, *Gulliver's Travels* (The Heritage Press, 1940), 22.
5. Molly Glick, "Phone Notifications Are Messing with Your Brain," *Discover*, April 29, 2022, https://www.discovermagazine.com/technology/phone-notifications-are-messing-with-your-brain.
6. Gloria Mark et al., "The Cost of Interrupted Work: More Speed and Stress," University of California, Irvine, accessed December 30, 2024, https://ics.uci.edu/~gmark/chi08-mark.pdf.
7. "Staying Focused in the Era of Digital Distractions," Harvard Health Publishing, June 6, 2020, https://www.health.harvard.edu/staying-healthy/staying-focused-in-the-era-of-digital-distractions.
8. Ann Pietrangelo, "How Does Dopamine Affect the Body?" Healthline, November 5, 2019, https://www.healthline.com/health/dopamine-effects.
9. Anne-Marie Slaughter, *Unfinished Business: Women, Men, Work, Family* (Random House, 2015), xvii.
10. Slaughter, *Unfinished Business*, 20.
11. Greg McKeown, *Essentialism: The Disciplined Pursuit of Less* (Crown Currency, 2014), 5.
12. "decide," Online Etymology Dictionary, accessed October 18, 2024, https://www.etymonline.com/word/decide.

Chapter 4: Live in Your Season

Epigraph: Elisabeth Elliot, *Let Me Be a Woman* (Tyndale, 1976), 104, ebook.
1. "culture," Online Etymology Dictionary, accessed October 21, 2024, https://www.etymonline.com/word/culture.
2. Ashlei Woods, "Putting the Basket in the Water: Trusting God in the Next Phase of Your Child's Life," Bridge Christian Church, July 5, 2016, https://bridgechristian.wordpress.com/2016/07/05/putting-the-basket-in-the-water-trusting-god-in-the-next-phase-of-your-childs-life/.

NOTES

Chapter 5: Choose Your Hard

Epigraph: St. Francis of Assisi
1. Tim Farris, "Derek Sivers on Developing Confidence, Finding Happiness, and Saying No to Millions (#125)," Tim Farris, December 14, 2015, https://tim.blog/2015/12/14/derek-sivers-on-developing-confidence-finding-happiness-and-saying-no-to-millions/.

Chapter 6: Just Start

Epigraph: Jeff Manion, *Dream Big, Think Small* (Zondervan, 2017), 21.
1. Jamie Erickson, "10 Minute Power Tasks for Homeschool Moms," *Learning Well Journal*, Spring 2022, 51–52.

Chapter 7: Move the Needle

Epigraph: Seneca, *On the Shortness of Life*, trans. C. D. N. Costa (Penguin, 2005), 1–2.
1. Megan Marples, "Decision Fatigue Drains You of Your Energy to Make Thoughtful Choices. Here's How to Get it Back," CNN Health, April 21, 2022, https://www.cnn.com/2022/04/21/health/decision-fatigue-solutions-wellness.
2. Charles Duhigg, *The Power of Habit* (Random House, 2012), xvi.
3. Samuel Johnson, "No. 178, November 30, 1751," in *The Rambler: A Periodical Paper* (Jones & Company, 1825), 304.
4. Simon Holland (@simoncholland), "No one is full of more false hope than a parent with a new chore chart," X, May 31, 2023, https://x.com/simoncholland/status/1663996951430348803?mx=2.
5. Phillippa Lally et al., "How Are Habits Formed: Modelling Habit Formation in the Real World," *European Journal of Social Psychology* 40, no. 6 (2009): 998–1009, https://doi.org/10.1002/ejsp.674.
6. Dan Diamond, "Just 8% of People Achieve Their New Year's Resolutions. Here's How They Do It," *Forbes*, January 1, 2013, https://www.forbes.com/sites/dandiamond/2013/01/01/just-8-of-people-achieve-their-new-years-resolutions-heres-how-they-did-it/.
7. Duncan Haughey, "A Brief History of SMART Goals," ProjectSmart, December 13, 2014, https://www.projectsmart.co.uk/smart-goals/brief-history-of-smart-goals.php.
8. Cal Newport, *Deep Work* (Grand Central Publishing, 2016), 42.
9. "The Impact of Interruptions," UC Berkeley: People & Culture, accessed January 1, 2025, https://hr.berkeley.edu/grow/grow-your-community/wisdom-caf%C3%A9-wednesday/impact-interruptions.

Chapter 8: Gather the Right People

Epigraph: Proverbs 13:20

1. The Editors of Encyclopedia Britannica, "Sea of Galilee," *Encyclopedia Britannica*, accessed January 1, 2025, https://www.britannica.com/place/Sea-of-Galilee.
2. "JetStream Max: 'A Funny Bath'—The Dead Sea," National Oceanic and Atmospheric Administration, March 28, 2023, https://www.noaa.gov/jetstream/dead-max.
3. "G3870 - parakaleō - Strong's Greek Lexicon (KJV)," Blue Letter Bible, accessed January 1, 2025, https://www.blueletterbible.org/lexicon/g3870/kjv/tr/0-1/.
4. Jamie Erickson (@unlikely_homeschool), "We live in an age when theology can be ordered to suit our individual preferences," Instagram, June 8, 2022, https://www.instagram.com/p/CejExFnLAsf/?hl=en.

Chapter 9: Let Them Go to Let Them Grow

Epigraph: Peter Walsh, *It's All Too Much* (Free Press, 2007), 27.

1. Gopal K. Singh, "Child Mortality in the United States, 1935–2007: Large Racial and Socioeconomic Disparities Have Persisted Over Time," A 75th Anniversary Publication, Health Resources and Services Administration, Maternal and Child Health Bureau (U.S. Department of Health and Human Services, 2010), 2.
2. Christopher Ingraham, "There's Never Been a Safer Time to Be a Kid in America," *The Washington Post*, April 14, 2015, https://www.washingtonpost.com/news/wonk/wp/2015/04/14/theres-never-been-a-safer-time-to-be-a-kid-in-america/.
3. Janis Wolak et al., "Child Victims of Stereotypical Kidnappings Known to Law Enforcement in 2011," *Juvenile Justice Bulletin*, June 1, 2016, https://ojjdp.ojp.gov/sites/g/files/xyckuh176/files/pubs/249249.pdf.
4. Andrea J. Sedlak et al., "Fourth National Incidence Studies of Missing, Abducted, Runaway and Thrownaway Children," National Criminal Justice Reference Service, May 29, 2022, https://www.ojp.gov/pdffiles1/nij/grants/304794.pdf, 29.
5. National Highway Traffic Safety Administration, "Traffic Safety Facts 2022 Data: Children," U.S. Department of Transportation, June 1, 2024, https://crashstats.nhtsa.dot.gov/Api/Public/Publication/813575, 1.

NOTES

6. Camilo Ortiz, "Treating Childhood Anxiety with a Mega-Dose of Independence," Profectus, March 14, 2023, https://profectusmag.com/treating-childhood-anxiety-with-a-mega-dose-of-independence/.
7. Jamie Erickson (@unlikely_homeschool), "Dear Mom whose son damaged the coach's property at the game last night," Instagram, June 11, 2024, https://www.instagram.com/p/C8FBHwAhpnO/?hl=en.
8. Jamie Erickson (@unlikely_homeschool), "Just like you, your kids are going to have fears," Instagram, July 29, 2019, https://www.instagram.com/p/B0gmiz7BKSz/?hl=en.
9. Syler Thomas and Steven Tighe, *Small-Group Leader's Quick Guide to (Almost) Everything* (Group Publishing, 2020), 116.
10. Jamie Erickson (@unlikely_homeschool), "Mamas, beware the lure of sticker charts, candy jars, or other dangling carrots," Instagram, February 9, 2023, https://www.instagram.com/p/Cocg13TrdsC/?hl=en.

Chapter 10: Loosen Your Grip

Epigraph: Corrie ten Boom, *Each New Day* (Revell, 2013), 103

1. "H7503 - *rāpâ* - Strong's Hebrew Lexicon (KJV)," Blue Letter Bible, accessed January 2, 2025, https://www.blueletterbible.org/lexicon/h7503/kjv/wlc/0-1/.

Women were made to give life—and they can do that right in their own homes.

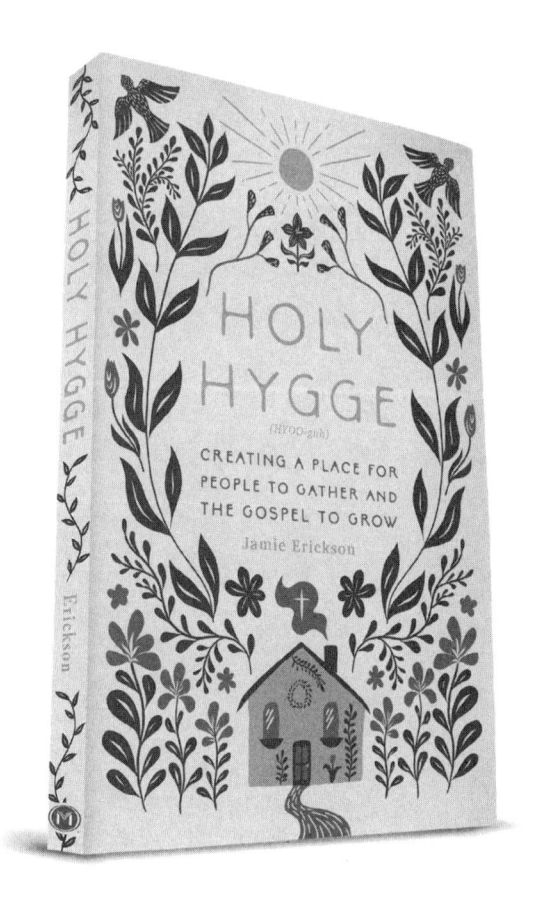

MOODY Publishers
From the Word to Life

Jamie unpacks seven tenets of the Danish practice *hygge*: hospitality, relationships, well-being, atmosphere, comfort, contentment, and rest. The external veneer of a lifestyle can become a life-giving home only with the gospel. *Holy Hygge* provides practical ideas for using hygge to gather people and introduce them to faith in Christ.

Also available as an eBook